THE GREAT LAKES GUIDEBOOK

George Cantor

THE GREAT LAKES GUIDEBOOK

WITHDRAWN

Lakes Ontario and Erie

Ann Arbor   The University of Michigan Press

In Canada: John Wiley & Sons Canada, Limited

New Edition 1985
Copyright © by The University of Michigan 1978, 1985
All rights reserved
Published in the United States of America by
The University of Michigan Press and simultaneously
in Rexdale, Canada, by John Wiley & Sons Canada, Limited
Manufactured in the United States of America

1988   1987   1986   1985   4   3   2

Library of Congress Cataloging in Publication Data

Cantor, George, 1941–
   The Great Lakes guidebook.

   Bibliography: p.
   Includes index.
   1. Ontario, Lake, Region (N.Y. and Ont.)—Description
and travel—Guide-books.   2. Erie, Lake, Region—
Description and travel—Guide-books.   I. Title.
F556.C36 1984   917.7'0433   84-13220
ISBN 0-472-06361-8 (pbk.)

Contents

Introduction

On a drizzly May morning in 1972 the *Stuart Cort* made its first voyage up the Detroit River. It was billed as the largest ship ever built on the Great Lakes, and there were a few short articles and a picture in the local papers to announce its passing.

A friend of mine was then employed as a speechwriter for the mayor of Detroit and one of the job's benefits was a cubicle of an office overlooking the river. He invited me up to share a lunchtime repast and watch the *Cort* go by, and I accepted, mostly because things were slow that day around lunchtime.

As we waited by the window on that murky day, an astonishing scene began unfolding far below us. Offices were letting out for the midday break and the streets leading to the river suddenly had jammed with people. They crowded along every open point on the riverfront, huddled under umbrellas and damp rain gear. We looked around and saw that in adjacent buildings every window with a river view was filled with people.

The drizzle became a shower, and the clock moved on to 12:30. Yet no one left. Everyone patiently watched the river. It was as if they were reaffirming some old, half-forgotten bond between them and the river. Shut off for years behind warehouses and railroad tracks and parking garages, the river still called to a city that had turned its back to it. The river could still compel the people to return to the city's source, its point of origin.

Finally, far down the river, around the great bend it makes to the south and past the Ambassador Bridge to Canada, came the *Cort*. Surrounded by an escort of light craft that frolicked around the giant ship like minnows around a sturgeon, the *Cort* made its majestic way past the city and the waiting throngs on shore. There may have been a few shouts and some hand waving, but most of the watchers simply stood in silence as it went by. The *Cort* passed from sight and the wet crowds dispersed almost instantly. In less than five minutes the streets were nearly empty and the rain spattered down on bare pavement. But for one hour in May, at least, an ancient bond had been acknowledged.

An even broader acknowledgement was made in the autumn of 1976 when a most unlikely record began working its way up the charts. It was an unusually long, haunting ballad about the wreck of a freighter in a howling November gale on Lake Superior. The song became one of the top hits of the year, not only in the Great Lakes area but in cities as far away as the Pacific Coast. People who had never even laid eyes on the Lakes listened in fascination to the chilling tale. For Canadian musician Gordon Lightfoot, who composed and performed "The Wreck of the *Edmund Fitzgerald,*" the hit must have been the most baffling of his successful career. He was no stranger to the pop charts and had proven to have a firm grasp on the elements of popular musical taste. But songs about shipwrecks are not generally gold-record material. Why should the *Fitzgerald* rise from its watery grave to ascend the record charts?

The ship had gone down in Whitefish Bay in 1975, about a year before the song was released. It was one of the most terrible and mysterious disasters of recent years on the Lakes. Pleasure boaters shuddered as they read the news. The gentle lakes that had buoyed their tiny crafts in summer had turned killer under the bleak skies of November. Across two nations they tried to imagine the incalculable power that could crumple a giant freighter as if it were a popsicle stick. The story remained on the front page of newspapers for about a week, then slowly faded from sight. But it remained much longer, submerged in the nightmare level of consciousness, to be called forth many months later by a song.

Evidently there is a wide appeal to the lore and drama of the Great Lakes, a deep fascination that can be tapped by a Gordon

Lightfoot. Most of the time, though, we treat the Lakes almost off-handedly. Those of us who live within 50 miles of their shores—which includes an enormous percentage of the total population of the United States and Canada—seem to take them for granted. It takes something like a special event or a disaster to remind us of their presence. Well, distance does lend enchantment they say, and a journey to Singapore probably beats the blazes out of a drive to Benton Harbor. Nonetheless, the familiar has its appeal. The unexpected beauty nearby that you never noticed before or the intriguing slice of history that occurred at your doorstep is as much a part of the travel experience as a week in Paris; and in their way equally as satisfying.

The Lakes are the perfect example of the wonder close at hand that we simply overlook. I know of few sights more thrilling than the lights of a giant freighter as it slips soundlessly past a great city at night. Or the first glimpse of blue water through the trees as the highway nears a lake. I am always surprised at how exciting that can be.

When I hear people who should know better complain about the dull scenery and lackluster history of the Midwest, and then learn that they have never been to Mackinac or Put-in-Bay, I am saddened. When I find that they have never stood on a Lake Superior bluff with the pines singing in the wind behind them, I am amused. There are landscapes of water, shore, and sky on the Lakes that compare favorably to any vista I have ever known. Yet there are those who will travel thousands of miles to take in scenery of approximate grandeur, return home full of snapshots and adjectives and never know what they're missing just a day's drive away. Or maybe they just have to be reminded. That is one purpose of this book.

Then there is the aftermath of the environmental awakening. The attention focused on the scandalous conditions in much of the Lakes system has resulted in stringent new pollution laws and controls. Miracles have been worked in the space of a decade. Some areas of the Lakes now enjoy cleaner water than at anytime in the last half century. Treatment plants are making a measurable impact on sewage and detergents dumped into the Lakes. (By the mid-70s, though, a new danger—concentrations of the chemical compound PCB, used in plastics and many other items—had been discovered in the Lakes' fish.) The patient is far from cured but the prognosis is improving. Except for a few trouble spots, the Upper Lakes are faring well. Ontario is described as holding its own by the international commission charged with overseeing the Lakes' environment. Even Erie, officially pronounced dead by the media during the height of the horror stories, has improved and may yet recover. But the initial publicity had a long-lasting effect. Once the public was alerted, it was hard to persuade people that the Lakes were improving. In areas removed from the Lakes, the Great Lakes were scratched off vacation lists and were never returned. Many travelers have not been back for years or have never seen the Lakes at all. This book is also meant for them.

Each of the five Great Lakes has its own personality, a set of characteristics that are apparent to those who sail their waters or who spend any length of time on their shores.

Lake Superior is the largest body of fresh water on the globe. It covers an area larger than the state of Maine, a total of 31,800 square miles. Its scenery matches its size. Superior is rimmed by hills and rugged bluffs, the most spectacular landscapes on the Lakes, and some of the grandest in the hemisphere. It is the *Gitche Gumee* of the Chippewas, the "laughing big sea water" of Longfellow's *Hiawatha*. But to the French it was *supérieur*. The bustling harbors at its western end—Duluth-Superior and Thunder Bay—send the freighters away full of grain and ore, making the lake a vital segment in the economy of two nations. These ports, however, are the only cities of any size on Superior's shores. Its largest island is Isle Royale, a U.S. national park and wilderness preserve. Other major geographic features are the Apostle Islands, Wisconsin, now a national lakeshore; the Pictured Rocks, also a national lakeshore, in Michigan; and the long, hooked arm of the ruggedly beautiful Keweenaw Peninsula of Michigan. The lake empties into the St. Marys River at the twin cities of Sault Ste. Marie. The Soo Locks there carry twice the traffic of the Panama Canal.

STATISTICS OF THE GREAT LAKES

Lakes	Length mi. km.	Breadth mi. km.	Size sq. mi. km.²	Greatest Depth ft. m.	Largest Cities
Superior	350 / 560	160 / 256	31,800 / 82,362	1,333 / 406	Thunder Bay, Ontario / Duluth, Minnesota / Superior, Wisconsin
Huron	206 / 330	183 / 293	23,010 / 59,595	750 / 229	Sarnia, Ontario / Port Huron, Michigan / Bay City, Michigan
Michigan	307 / 491	118 / 189	22,400 / 58,016	923 / 281	Chicago, Illinois / Milwaukee, Wisconsin / Gary, Indiana
Erie	241 / 386	57 / 91	9,910 / 25,667	210 / 64	Cleveland, Ohio / Buffalo, New York / Toledo, Ohio
Ontario	193 / 309	53 / 85	7,550 / 19,555	802 / 244	Toronto, Ontario / Hamilton, Ontario / Rochester, New York

Lake Huron comes next, the lake first seen by Europeans but the one that has remained least developed. Samuel de Champlain reached its shores in 1615. He had worked his way from Montreal along the Ottawa River, overland to Lake Nipissing and then along the French River to its outlet at the lake. He took this rather circuitous route west because the hostile Iroquois controlled the southern approaches. The existence of Lakes Erie and Ontario was then only a vague rumor. Even with this head start, Huron has remained far from the most heavily traveled roads. The site at which Champlain first saw the lake remains inaccessible by automobile. Lake Huron's largest city, Sarnia, Ontario, has a population of about 60,000. The only other significant pocket of industry is concentrated on Saginaw Bay, which contributes whatever pollution the lake suffers. It is the second largest of the Lakes and the most irregularly shaped. Its massive eastern arm, Georgian Bay, is cut off from the rest of the lake by Manitoulin Island, the largest island on the Lakes. Other islands shield the North Channel. There are two units of Georgian Bay

Islands National Park in Canada, one near Midland and the other at the tip of the slender Bruce Peninsula, near Tobermory. Mackinac Island, one of the stateliest resorts in the States, guards the western approach to Lake Huron at the Straits of Mackinac.

Lake Michigan is separated from Lake Huron only by a narrow strait. The two lakes lie at the same distance above sea level and are virtual twins in size. But Michigan is a lake with a split personality. At its southern end, unlike Huron, it supports one of the most intensive concentrations of industrial wealth and population in the world. Chicago, the pivotal metropolis of the Lakes, occupies its southwestern corner. The band of development continues eastward around the Calumet district of Indiana and northward to Milwaukee, another booming port and industrial center. But where the suburbs of the Wisconsin city end, the North begins and Lake Michigan becomes a resort-studded jewel. Its waves lap at some of the richest vacation property in the Midwest. Green Bay, on the Wisconsin shore, has the Door Peninsula, and on the east the two Traverse Bays, Grand and Little, are lined with showplaces. Nearby is the Sleeping Bear Dunes National Lakeshore. Michigan is the only Great Lake entirely within the boundaries of the United States, but its largest island, Beaver, once was ruled by a king—albeit a self-proclaimed monarch.

The accumulated flows of Lakes Michigan and Huron empty into the St. Clair River at the cities of Sarnia and Port Huron. At the far end they flow into Lake St. Clair, a sort of Great Lake, junior grade. At 460 square miles it is somewhat bigger than a pond but not in the same league as its enormous neighbors. Its Canadian shoreline is mostly undeveloped and Walpole Island is occupied by an Indian reservation. Detroit's suburbs sprawl along its southwestern end. At Belle Isle it meets the Detroit River, busiest inland waterway in the world and scene of industrialization beyond compare.

Lake Erie is the shallowest, busiest, oldest, and dirtiest of the Lakes. Sailors distrust it. The lake is shaped like a saucer and when storms come out of the west it can be a treacherous body of water. One of these gales can cause a thirteen-foot difference in water level at opposite ends of the lake and raise waves of frightening size. With an average depth of just fifty-eight feet Erie is also especially susceptible to industrial pollution and because of pollution it has suffered more severely than any other lake. Its southern shoreline is covered with major ports, from Toledo to Buffalo, and industrial discharges from Detroit alone almost succeeded in killing it. The lake is improving but is by no stretch of the imagination clean. Still, it supports major resort areas around Ohio's Sandusky Bay and the Presque Isle Peninsula of Pennsylvania. In contrast to the American shore, the Canadian side of Erie is almost empty, with only small resorts and fishing towns breaking the long stretches of solitude. Point Pelee and Long Point, both major wildlife sanctuaries and bird refuges, are the main landmarks. Pelee Island, largest in the lake, belongs to Canada and is primarily agricultural.

Erie empties into the churning Niagara River, which thunders over its escarpment a few miles on to form one of the world's great natural wonders. A few miles beyond Niagara Falls, the river passes through a tumultuous gorge before peacefully emerging into the last of the Lakes.

Lake Ontario is the least Great Lake, covering only 7,550 square miles, which is still a larger area than the state of New Jersey. But it is the second deepest, with an average sounding of 283 feet. Its depth results in a strong moderating influence over the adjacent countryside's climate, and one of the great fruit belts of North America is situated around its littoral. The western end of the lake is Ontario's most densely populated region. Toronto, second largest city in the country, and Hamilton, one of Canada's greatest manufacturing centers, present a solid belt of intensive development. On the American side, however, Rochester is the only city of significant size. The shoreline is quite regular, with only the mass of Quinte's Isle breaking into the lake from the north. There are no islands of any size in Lake Ontario, aside from the farthest eastern corner. There Wolfe and Amherst, Ontario, guard the entrance to the St. Lawrence River at Kingston, eastern limit to the Lakes.

From Duluth, Minnesota, to Kingston, Ontario, is a journey of 1,160 miles through the world's largest freshwater system, the largest inland water transportation network—the superlatives go on and on. You might consider this: The Great Lakes system contains sixty-seven trillion gallons of water, and much of it is even drinkable.

In terms of geological time, the Great Lakes are rank upstarts. They began taking shape about 18,000 years ago, the end product of North America's final age of glacial activity. It was called the Wisconsin Age, because the ice reached to what is now the southern limits of that state. As the glaciers started their long retreat, ancient stream valleys were uncovered and slowly began filling with meltwater and rain. Lakes formed in the area of Chicago and the Maumee Valley, both bodies of water draining into the Mississippi River. As the ice moved farther north the patterns changed. The lakes twisted into new shapes and sent their waters over newly formed drainage routes. Lake Erie and the southern portion of Lake Michigan had reached an approximation of their present forms about 10,000 years ago. Lake Ontario was shaped about 7,000 years ago. The Upper Lakes assumed their present outline a mere 3,000 years ago.

We have said previously that Champlain was the first European to see the Lakes, but that may not be strictly true. A shadowy figure named Étienne Brulé, sent out by Champlain to scout the area, may actually have reached the Lakes as early as 1612. It is hard to say. Brulé left no records. He was illiterate and was the first of the voyageurs to successfully adapt to the ways of the Indians. Eventually he was killed by them in the wilderness, after ranging from Lake Ontario to Isle Royale. He is, however, given credit for being the first European to see Lake Superior.

Twenty years after Champlain's expedition, Jean Nicolet explored Lake Michigan, reaching the site of Green Bay, Wisconsin. By 1631, two Jesuit priests, Fathers Jogues and Rambault, had established missions there and on Lake Superior, at Ashland, Wisconsin, and the Soo. Not until 1669 was the last of the Lakes discovered. Louis Joliet and Robert LaSalle entered Lake Erie a few days apart that summer from opposite directions. In another four years, Joliet and Father Marquette would discover the route from the Lakes to the Mississippi River, and Fort Frontenac would be established as a permanent settlement at the mouth of the St. Lawrence River.

Finally, in 1679, LaSalle embarked on the crowning epic of Great Lakes discovery. Aboard his ship, the *Griffon,* he sailed across Erie, up the Detroit River and around Huron into Michigan, finally disembarking at Green Bay. The voyage opened up the southern route to the Upper Lakes and clarified the geographic relationship between the two segments. LaSalle went on to trace the Mississippi River to the Gulf of Mexico. The *Griffon* was sent home to Lake Erie and on the way back it vanished. Several museums around the Lakes display bits and pieces of what is thought to be the wreckage of the ship. But that is only guesswork. No one knows what happened to the ship or exactly where it went down. On that mysterious note the great discoveries on the Lakes ended and the age of settlement began.

It took the War of 1812 to establish the boundary between the United States and Canada in the Great Lakes area. In 1817 the border was settled by the Rush-Bagot Agreement and it has not been changed since.

Crossing this frontier is usually an uncomplicated, rapid procedure. No documents are required for citizens of either country, but it is advisable to carry some proof of citizenship, such as a copy of a birth certificate or voter registration card. Naturalized citizens should carry their certificates of naturalization and aliens must have their registration cards.

Motorists should have proof of car ownership and insurance coverage with them. Most personal items may be taken across the border without trouble, but rifles and expensive camera equipment should be registered at the border. No handguns are permitted in Canada.

Dogs may cross the border if their owners present a certificate that the animal has been vaccinated against rabies in the last year. A description of the animal must accompany the certificate. Cats may cross freely.

For complete customs information, the traveler should request information, in advance, from the Customs Office in either Washington, D.C., or Ottawa, Ontario.

All of which brings us to this book.

It has been my experience as a travel editor that travel books fall roughly into two major categories. There are the personalized books of essays and observations, which may be great fun to read but not much help when it comes right down to planning a trip. Then there are the nuts-and-bolts sorts of listings, which have all the facts and figures but are about as readable as the Yellow Pages.

I have tried to stake out a middle ground. It is my hope that the essays in this book are written in a manner that will entertain. But I also intend for this book to be used as a planner and an on-the-road reference guide.

It is a selective guidebook. I have made no attempt to catalog every sight and attraction on the shoreline of the Great Lakes. I did endeavor, though, to list the best and the most significant. They are the places that reflect the long and colorful history of the area, with appeal that is unique to the Lakes. When I included an amusement park, for instance, I did so because the park had been there for over a century and was a genuine chunk of Great Lakes history, not because it was a good amusement park. There are dozens of those in this cookie-cutter world of ours. This one, however, had roots in the land. It could be situated in no other place but Cedar Point, Ohio.

At the beginning of each chapter, there is an introductory essay about the particular area being explored. It will examine some of the features that influenced the area's historical development and the special qualities that can be found there.

Offered next are three attractions that I have selected as being the best in the area. If you are traveling through, these are the things you should make a special effort to see. Some of them are among the best-known sights on the continent, others are rarely publicized outside their immediate locale. But they are all top-notch attractions. These three sights are discussed in depth, and several are accompanied by useful maps.

After that follows a section we have called "Other Things to See." They are listed in about the order in which you would encounter them were you to drive across the area. A few of these sights are marked with boldface numbers. This indicates that while they do not quite rank with the "Top Three" in the area, they are nonetheless unusually worthwhile and significant attractions. The others on the list can be seen during a stay of a few days in the area or may appeal to special interests. Other maps in this section have insets showing greater detail of the major cities in the area not otherwise visible in the larger map.

A section called "Side Trips" suggests interesting things to see within a 50-mile drive of the lakeshore. Following that, there is a list of major state and provincial parks in the area, especially those with lakefront recreational facilities. If overnight camping is permitted, the number of tent sites is given.

Finally, since the time span of a vacation can measure anywhere from a few stolen hours to a leisurely holiday lasting weeks, there are two lists at the end of each chapter outlining strategies for a short weekend visit and for a week-long stay. This is a new feature of the book, designed to help you make the most of whatever vacation time you do have.

That, in brief, is our book.
Read it and enjoy it. Most of all, use it.

The accumulated fury of four Great Lakes crashes over the brink of Niagara Falls.

The Niagara Frontier

It is best to approach Niagara Falls carefully, from behind, along the parkway on the Canadian side. A few miles upstream, where the two branches of the Niagara River join beyond Grand Island, it is a broad, almost lakelike stream, without a hint of the thundering passion just a short distance in its future. Once past the village of Chippawa, the flow accelerates. There are passages of white water. There has been so much diversion to power plants that it is impossible to tell what this stretch of river looked like in an earlier age. The water is rushing now. A curve of the road is rounded and all at once the river in front of you vanishes. Where its course should be, a white mist rises instead. You cannot hear the roar yet. There is only the mist hovering above the precipice, more terrifying than any roar imaginable.

Niagara Falls may be the single most heavily developed tourist attraction on the North American continent. Its days as a honeymoon capital are behind it, but the place still holds a popular image so familiar that it approaches cliché. The sophisticated, jet-age traveler speaks of it with condescension. You will never stop a cocktail party cold by regaling the guests with your trip to Niagara. They may even think you a bit odd for getting excited about the place.

But do not underestimate its power. Niagara Falls is still a stunning, terrifying thing to see. It is always amusing to see some obscure, ribbon-thin cataract billed as being "three times higher than Niagara." That misses the point completely. It is not Niagara's height (only 182 feet on the American side, 176 on the Canadian) that is the attraction. It is that enormous volume of water, the accumulated fury of four Great Lakes, crashing over the brink. The figures say it is a volume of 200,000 cubic feet of water every second. The figures cannot convey what this onrush looks like—or what it sounds like when it batters against the rocks at the base.

The first European to see Niagara supposedly was Father Louis Hennepin. He had heard about the falls from the Indians and asked to be taken to them in 1678. When he got around to writing about his experiences in North America five years later, he described the falls as being 600 feet high. It is easy to see how he could have made the mistake. When you see something like Niagara for the first time, it sure looks 600 feet high. An accompanying engraving of this phenomenon excited enormous curiosity about the falls, and all the other remarkable sights of the New World, across Europe. Later visitors improved on Hennepin's measurements; one observer even estimated they were 800 feet high. Much of the eighteenth-century descriptive material on the falls was, in fact, taken up with a debate over just how high they were. Once that was settled the business of tourism proceeded.

The War of 1812 intervened, though. The Niagara frontier was a particularly strategic and especially bloody battleground. Invading forces passed back and forth over the international border. Forts were taken and retaken on both sides, cities torched, and men slaughtered. The residue of bitterness lasted many years afterward on this segment of the U.S.-Canada boundary.

Within a decade of the war's close, however, the falls had become a noted tourist attraction. It was an obligatory stop for European gentlemen doing America and an excursion point for nearby residents. Now that everyone was satisfied as to the falls' height, the next question was how best to view them. The Terrapin Tower was constructed in 1833 on Goat Island near the brink of the Canadian Falls. It stood there for forty years, the forerunner of the bewildering agglomeration of viewing towers that dot the landscape in the falls' vicinity today. In 1846 the original *Maid of the Mist* began its runs upon the mangled waters to the base of the falls. Stairs had been carved into the cliff face on the American side as early as 1818 and by midcentury Table Rock had been constructed as a viewing platform on the Canadian shore.

As the crowds grew so did the sideshows. A boatload of animals was sent crashing over the falls in 1827 for the edification of thousands of spectators. Sam Patch dove into the river below the falls. Charles Blondin walked a tightrope across the gorge in 1859 and repeated the stunt with various embellishments all of that summer and the next. That brought on a whole assortment of acrobats to strut and prance across the river. The only casualty came when one of them tried to do it at night while drunk. A woman made the walk in 1876. That seemed to cap off that particular craze, but ten years later Carlisle D. Graham began a whole new one by becoming the first man to run the falls in a barrel.

The common thread uniting these spectacles was the sense of awe and terror onlookers felt at the sight of the falls. But by the end of the Civil War that sense was being mitigated somewhat by the carnival atmosphere surrounding the area. The place was a mess. Tourists were being swindled, con men and peddlers crowded the streets, mills and factories defaced the riverbanks.

Sentiment for a remedy originated in New York in 1869, but it was not until sixteen years later that a bill authorizing a 415-acre park on the American side was signed into law. Canada, goaded into action, passed its own legislation the same year. In 1887 it enacted an even more ambitious program, the nucleus of the magnificent system of landscaped parks that eradicated the last traces of blight on its side of the falls. It happened just in time, too. Formation of the Parks Commission coincided with the development of hydroelectric power systems at the falls. The power plants then were fitted into a framework of parks rather than operating without aesthetic controls.

The American side has lagged behind Ontario. But in recent years New York also has substantially improved its appearance. The last pocket of the old sideshow world is on the Canadian side on Clifton Hill, a block-long assortment of freak shows, magic displays, and wax museums. Restricted as it is to this one area, it even has a certain tacky charm. Most of the attractions there are extravagantly overpriced, though.

The ridge over which the falls drop, the Niagara Escarpment, continues west into Canada. It eventually cuts across the entire Province of Ontario, ending in the Georgian Bay. The strip of land lying between Lake Ontario and the escarpment is shielded from the prevailing winds, and as a result, is the richest fruit-growing area in the province. Canada's wine industry is centered around the St. Catharines area. Drives along the escarpment are particularly lovely in spring when the orchards are in bloom.

St. Catharines also is the outlet of the Welland Canal which carries shipping around the falls from Lake Erie to Lake Ontario. Completed in 1829 the canal is a major link in the St. Lawrence Seaway. It runs for 27.6 miles to Port Colborne and climbs a total of 326 feet over the escarpment.

At the head of the Niagara Peninsula is the great steel manufacturing city of Hamilton, Ontario. For an industrial city, though, it is a surprisingly attractive place. The escarpment is known locally as "The Mountain" and runs right through the middle of Hamilton, giving the place a split-level personality. Drives along the ridge, looking out over the city and its harbor, are impressive and Hamilton also has a fine system of parks and gardens. It is Ontario's second largest city, albeit a bit overshadowed by the proximity of Toronto, just 35 miles down the lake.

The Falls

There are some wet blankets who predict that in a few thousand years or so Niagara Falls will be nothing but a huge whirlpool at the mouth of Lake Erie. The falls already have retreated 7 miles up the river from where they were formed 12,000 years ago and the process of erosion, the tumbling water wearing away the rock underneath, pushes it back about three feet a year. They are about one-sixth of a mile away from where Father Hennepin first saw them in 1678. Even in a single lifetime the American falls have changed dramatically in appearance. Huge rockslides in 1931 and 1954 have piled up a mound of talus at the base. Diversion of water for electrical power has also dropped the pool at the base of the falls some twenty feet, exposing more rock. The difference between the way the falls look now and a photograph from fifty or so years ago is striking. An international commission, formed in 1967 to study the situation, concluded that the natural erosion process should not be interfered with, but that further major rock falls should be prevented and that some of the talus probably should be cleared away at some unspecified time.

By the time the falls have made their way backward to Buffalo harbor, these pages will be dust. While the geologists wrestle with these problems, our question is what is the best way to see the falls right now? Take your choice. You can stand at the brink. You can stand at the base. You can take a boat. You can take an elevator. You can see them from a tower. You can see them from a helicopter. We will take the viewpoints in order.

From the Brink

The Canadian side offers the best viewpoints. It also has the more attractive parks. From this angle you are facing the American Falls head-on and can see the great horseshoe of the Canadian Falls from several different perspectives. The gardens of Queen Victoria Park begin at the brink of the Canadian cascade and the falls never look quite so appealing as when viewed through a foreground of flowers. The 196-acre park is famous for its daffodil displays in spring and also contains formal gardens, a rock garden, and a greenhouse. In the midst of it is the Victoria Park Restaurant, a fine place for "eating the scenery," fixing the landscape in your mind by stimulating several senses at once. At least, that is sixteenth-century sculptor Benvenuto Cellini's theory.

Prospect Point on the American side is also a noteworthy view, catching the rush of the falls in profile. There is a bridge to pleasantly landscaped Goat Island, which lies between the two falls. Viewmobile rides are available on both sides of the border for those who do not care to walk to the major points of interest.

From the Base

Now we are getting somewhere. You can feel it as you enter the dressing room and begin covering every part of your body in rainwear. When you have to put on a special costume to make a trip, that is adventure. Both sides have wonderful excursions to the base of the roaring cataracts and there is probably no better way of experiencing the crushing power, the awesome crash of the water.

Both trips take you to the base of the falls by elevator. At Table Rock, on the Canadian side, you walk through a tunnel to the viewing platform. Keep your camera under protective cover; the lens will be soaked instantly in the heavy spray. A series of passageways leads to the other points behind the falls, but all you can see is the water plunging past the opening in the rock. You can get the same effect by standing in a bathroom shower. The American side, Cave of the Winds, has a more extensive system of wooden walkways in the open which actually do lead to different perspectives. Either trip is thrilling, the best way to see the falls. Cave of the Winds closes from mid-October to May 1; Table Rock remains open all year.

Maid of the Mist

The story of the Indian maid, who was sent over the falls as a sacrifice and can be discerned in the mist by the imaginative, first appeared in print in an 1851 guidebook. By the turn of the

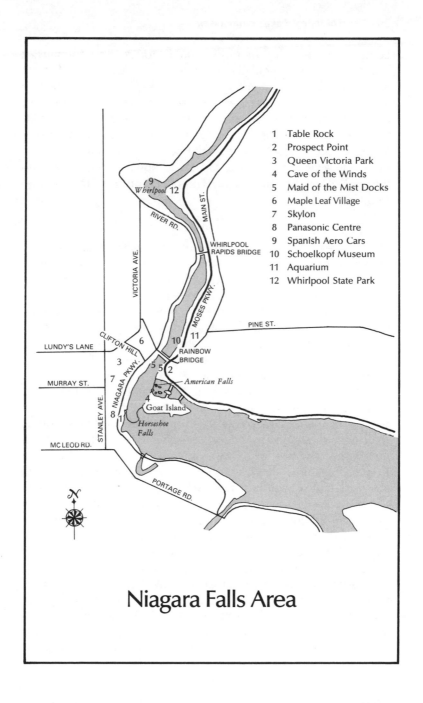

1   Table Rock
2   Prospect Point
3   Queen Victoria Park
4   Cave of the Winds
5   Maid of the Mist Docks
6   Maple Leaf Village
7   Skylon
8   Panasonic Centre
9   Spanish Aero Cars
10 Schoelkopf Museum
11 Aquarium
12 Whirlpool State Park

Niagara Falls Area

century it was one of the most popular stories about the falls. It probably is a romanticized corruption of a more complex Seneca myth in which the maid is prevented from killing herself in the falls by a god. Whatever the case, the little boats named for the misty maiden leave on their trips to the base of the falls from both sides of the border. On the American side, an elevator runs from Prospect Point to the boat landing. On the Canadian side an incline railway takes you down to the dock from the foot of gaudy Clifton Hill. The boats run from mid-May to mid-October.

The Towers

The outbreak of viewing towers in the Niagara area is now at epidemic proportions. There are no fewer than four of them, varying widely in height and ambience, to assist viewers in seeing the falls from the grand perspective. Three of them are on the Canadian side including the two most elaborate—Panasonic Centre and the Skylon. The single American tower is situated at Prospect Point. The down car on the elevator there takes you to the *Maid of the Mist;* the up car ascends to a 282-foot high observation deck. Open all year.

But that is only a tower. The three facilities on the Canadian side are family entertainment centers, if you please. The newest of them is Maple Leaf Village, an enclosed shopping mall with an attached outdoor amusement complex, located at the base of Clifton Hill, near the entrance to the Rainbow Bridge. It features views not only from a 350-foot high tower in the mall, but also from a ferris wheel in the amusement park. Various combination tickets for the attractions are on sale there. The outdoor portion is open June 15 to September 15. The indoor tower is open daily in the summer, 10:00 A.M. to 10:00 P.M., and on weekends only in the winter. Two other viewing towers dominate the skyline on the Canadian side. The Panasonic Centre (it is the one with longer windows) is the shorter of the two—by 135 feet if you measure from sea level, by 195 feet if you measure the height of the tower itself. It contains six decks at the top, a dining room with panoramic view, an aquarium with dolphin and sea lion shows, a wax museum, and the

Visitors to the looming Skylon tower can take in an all-encompassing view of Niagara Falls. *Photograph by Doris Scharfenberg.*

Waltzing Waters. One admission price covers all. The Skylon, tallest of the towers, has a revolving restaurant at the apex of its 520-foot high structure. There is also an indoor, bilevel shopping center and a children's ride area with indoor Ferris wheel.

Chopper
If the towers are just too tame for your taste, try the view from a helicopter. They leave from the American side at a base on Goat Island. In Canada, the Niagara Helicopter Tours has its offices on Victoria at River Road.

The falls are illuminated at night throughout the year. Many connoisseurs insist the best time of the year to view them is in the dead of winter when their churning power is frozen in icy majesty and the crowds have all gone home. Better dress warmly, though.

Niagara-on-the-Lake

One could start out by saying that this is the prettiest village in Ontario. But that probably understates the case. Totally removed from the hustle and pace of Niagara Falls, just a few miles along the river, Niagara-on-the-Lake dwells in another time, a different world. It is a world of vine-covered cottages and white picket fences and fudge shops and restaurants in century-old buildings. To stroll along Queen Street, its broad main thoroughfare, is to step into pure delight.

The first comparison that comes to mind is Carmel-by-the-Sea in California. But that is not fair. There is a hard edge to Carmel's quaintness. Its luxury boutiques and shops dispense goods far costlier than fudge. One is left with the sense that its architecture is Spanish Colonial because it is picturesque and good for business. The homes and shops of Niagara, though, bear genuine historic links. They stood here long before the merchants thought to trade on their appearance, not the other way around.

There is also the temptation to draw a comparison with a Cotswold village. There is, after all, a strong British feeling here. The place was settled by United Empire Loyalists who preferred starting again in a new place under the crown to living in post-revolutionary America. But the village could be located in no other country but Canada. Its traditions go back to the very birth of the country. Niagara-on-the-Lake simply is unique unto itself. No comparisons are necessary.

Since 1963 it has hosted the Shaw Festival, presenting the works of British playwright George Bernard Shaw in repertory every summer. That has served to introduce the village to a wider audience. Still, of the hundreds of thousands who flock to Niagara Falls every year, only a small fraction find their way to this spot where the Niagara River empties into Lake Ontario.

The location was always important strategically. For the French it was the link between the eastern and western halves of their vast colonial empire. For the British and later the Americans it controlled access to Lake Erie and the water passage to the Midwest. Both sides of the river here were fortified by the end of the eighteenth century.

Upper New York had been strongly Loyalist during the Revolution. Butler's Raiders, a Loyalist unit led by John Butler and his son Walter, spread fire and terror throughout the Mohawk Valley and into Pennsylvania. At the end of the hostilities, returning to their former homes was out of the question. So the Raiders crossed the Niagara and settled down on land granted to them by the crown to secure the largely unpopulated region that would become Ontario.

By 1792 enough people had moved into the area to force Britain into an administrative division of the Canadian colony. The future province of Ontario became Upper Canada with its capital in the lakeside village of Newark. John Graves Simcoe, the colony's first governor-general, recognized, however, that the capital was in a precarious position. It was too exposed to a sudden onslaught from the Americans across the river. He decided to move the seat of government to a more secure location. He chose the village of York. York would grow into the metropolis of Toronto. Newark would remain a village and become Niagara-on-the-Lake.

But first both villages would be burned down by American invaders during the War of 1812. Some historians believe that the burning of Washington, D.C., by the British in 1814 was done in retaliation for the wanton destruction of tiny Newark, rather than for the razing of York, which is the more widespread belief. (Still others think that it was the burning of Port Dover that brought the torch to Washington. It seemed to be a great war for burning cities.)

The burning of Niagara-on-the-Lake on December 10, 1813, was the last time history touched the place. The serenity of the intervening years is reflected in its streets. Still there are a few major sights to visit. The Niagara Historical Society Museum, with items belonging to Simcoe, General Isaac Brock, Canadian heroine Laura Secord, and many Loyalist families, supplies an admirable introduction to the town. Located two blocks south of the business district on Castlereagh Street, it is open between 1:00 and 7:00 from mid-May to mid-September; between 1:00 and 5:00 on Wednesday, Saturday, and Sunday the rest of the years. The Niagara Apothecary on Queen Street is an interesting reconstruction of a nineteenth-century pharmacy. The building actually was a pharmacy for ninety-eight years until 1964 and is now operated as a museum by the Ontario College of Pharmacy. It is open from mid-May to mid-September; the admission is free.

South of town is Fort George (see page 29) and the McFarland House, a good example of Georgian domestic architecture on the frontier. Parts of the home date to 1800 and it was used as a hospital during the War of 1812. Operated by the Niagara Parks Commission, it is closed Mondays and Tuesdays.

For the rest, it is best simply to walk the streets and drink in the flavor of this lovingly maintained village. Be sure and explore the side streets, too. By all means stroll over to Front Street and visit the park at the mouth of the river. Sit on the bluff and watch the river meet the lake, the boats dancing out to the open water, and the bulk of Fort Niagara across the stream. All combine to make it one of the most delightful vistas on the Lakes.

The War of 1812 on the Niagara

Thirty years after the end of the American Revolution, sentiment in the new republic for the annexation of Canada became irresistible. Most Americans, especially those in the new western lands, thought annexation would be a snap. They feared that the British and their Indian allies would continue to harass settlers in the Northwest unless driven from their Canadian bases. They also thought that with the British occupied elsewhere in the Napoleonic wars, the undermanned Canadians could not withstand an invasion and that former Americans who had moved to Canada would not resist very vigorously. There were, of course, other factors for the conflict. But the main impetus for the war came from the expansionist West and its representatives in Congress, the "War Hawks."

The battlegrounds of the war were spread over a wide section of the continent. But some of the most furious fighting was done along the banks of the Niagara River. To the Americans, this section of Canada seemed to hold the greatest promise of rapid conquest and strategic advantage. Instead, the Niagara campaign turned into two years of raids, burnings, and pitched battles. Trying to follow the events chronologically becomes a bit confusing from the traveler's viewpoint. So for the purpose of geographic clarity we will trace the various campaigns from a south-to-north direction along the Niagara Parkway.

Fort Erie
This outpost at the Lake Erie source of the Niagara began as a French trading post in 1750. The British fortified it fourteen years later in response to Pontiac's Rebellion, the aftermath of the French and Indian War. A violent winter storm destroyed that fort in 1779 when a huge ice mass smashed into it. A second fort was wiped out in precisely the same manner in 1803. The British, having finally learned their lesson, began construction of a third fort on a knoll about 100 yards from the riverbank site of the first two. This was a square masonry affair with four bastions.

An American force took the fort unopposed in 1813, held it

for thirteen days and then retreated across the river. But they returned 4,500 strong in July, 1814. The British garrison of 150 surrendered and the last major U.S. invasion of Canada was underway. Two days later as these troops advanced along the river they met British regulars at Chippawa. To the amazement of the British, the grey-clad troops of General Winfield Scott did not break before the regulars, the usual result of such encounters in the war. This time it was the British who left the field in full retreat. The victory was such a boost to American morale that the War Department ordered cadets at West Point henceforth to dress in the colors of Scott's brigade, the origin of the Military Academy's "Long Grey Line."

After a bloody standoff at Lundy's Lane (see below) the Americans returned to Fort Erie with the British in hot pursuit. On August 7, an eight-day bombardment of the fort began. The British then sent in a predawn assault on August 16. The main body was turned back but a detachment of 300 to 400 soldiers seized one of the bastions and turned the guns against the American defenders. Suddenly the powder magazine below the bastion exploded and the invaders were wiped out, ending the battle with 950 British dead. The campaign dwindled down to a series of raids and sorties. In November the Americans abandoned the fort and demolished it.

A monument erected in 1903 covers the mass grave of 153 soldiers from both sides whose remains were found on the grounds. The fort itself was restored in 1939 to its appearance of the war years. Guides dressed in the uniform of the British Eighth Regiment demonstrate period drills in the summer months. A museum is on the grounds, containing a history of the fort and artifacts found in the area. Open mid-May to mid-October; there is an admission charge.

Lundy's Lane

Just a few blocks from the holiday mood of Niagara Falls is a somber reminder of war's final accounting. In the Drummond Hill churchyard are the graves and monuments that mark the spot of the furious engagement that broke the last American incursion into Canada. The Americans, victorious at Chippawa, moved to the falls and turned west. The British had drawn up their lines on a rise along Lundy's Lane. In the ensuing battle, on July 25, 1813, both American generals, Scott and Jacob Brown, were wounded. The British were driven from their position, but American losses were so severe that they had to fall back to Chippawa. Next day the British reoccupied the heights and the exhausted Americans fell back to Fort Erie, unable to take the offensive again.

A monument and a few graves are all that remain on the site of one of the war's pivotal struggles. To get there, follow Highway 20 west from the falls to Drummond Avenue. The churchyard is on the south side of the road.

Queenston Heights
The American forces chose to make their first incursion into Canada against the village of Queenston, across the river from Lewiston, New York, below the falls. It was almost successful. But inspirational leadership on the British side and fragmented command among the Americans turned it into a rout. An advance force seized the Canadian bank and heights on the night of October 12, 1812. General Isaac Brock, fresh from his stunning triumph at Detroit, personally led a counterattack. He was killed at the head of his troops and by the following afternoon it appeared as if the Americans had secured their position. But the invaders had failed to fortify their position properly and reinforcements ordered up by Brock were able to outflank them. When General Stephen Van Rensselaer ordered American reserves from the far side of the river, though, the New York militiamen abruptly decided they were not bound to serve outside the boundaries of the state. They refused to cross over. The outnumbered Americans, panicked by Indian raids on their position, broke at the British charge. A retreat across the Niagara was impossible. Surrender was their only alternative.

The battle stiffened Canada's will to resist the invaders and also gave it a national hero and martyr in Brock. The impressive monument to the fallen general dominates the field. A walking tour of the battleground may be followed by a system of numbered cairns.

Fort George

Built in 1796 to protect the settlement of Newark, the fort was taken by an American amphibious assault on May 26, 1813. It was one of the best coordinated actions in the war on the American side. The British defenders escaped, however, and handed the Americans two sharp setbacks at Stoney Creek (just east of Hamilton) and Beaver Dams. That ended the offensive and Fort George was left with a small garrison. When a British force moved on it in December, the commander ordered a retreat across the river. But first his troops burned Newark. Inexplicably, he failed to burn the fort, too, and when the British arrived they were able to take over a virtually undamaged installation. There are now eleven restored buildings on the grounds. Open daily, mid-May to mid-October; there is an admission charge.

Fort Niagara

This is one of the most impressive military restorations in North America. Fort Niagara's importance preceded the War of 1812 by more than a century. The French recognized the strategic importance of the land it occupies very early. They made an unsuccessful attempt to fortify it as early as 1678. By holding the entrance to the Niagara River, they felt capable of sustaining communications within their sprawling colonial empire. It also gave them an outpost to confront the advancing tide of British colonization to the south. In 1726 Louis Joincare arrived here and informed the Iroquois that he was going to build a trading post. When the structure was finished, though, it had come out very much like a fort—a three-story stronghold with barracks and a gun deck on the top floor. His building, the "Castle," still stands on the grounds, one of the most historic structures west of the Mohawk Valley.

The fort was a target of primary importance in the French and Indian War and fell to the British after a long siege a few weeks before the capture of Quebec. During the Revolution it was the base for Butler's Raiders and remained in British hands for thirteen years after the end of hostilities, so reluctant were they to surrender the position.

After American forces burned Newark in 1813 and re-treated across the river from Fort George, this fort became the objective for the infuriated British command. Within a few days a swift attack across the frontier surprised the entire American sentry detachment. Undetected, the British stormed through the unguarded main gate and took the fort and its entire garrison within a matter of minutes. They lost 11 men in the attack; the Americans had 65 dead, 14 wounded, and 344 taken prisoner. The British followed this success with a series of raids across the New York frontier, culminating in an Indian massacre at Lewis-ton and the burning of Buffalo. The fort remained again in their hands until the end of the war. A memorial to the subsequent Rush-Bagot Treaty, which established the demilitarized U.S.-Canadian border, stands in the fort today.

A self-guiding walking tour takes the visitor through the medieval-looking main gate, around the blockhouses and ramparts, and into the Castle. An excellent museum explains the fort's historic and geographic significance. Costumed guides man the sentry posts in summer and put on drills and firearms demonstrations. It ranks with Fort Henry, Ontario, as the best attraction of its kind along the Lakes. Open daily all year; admission charge.

Other Things to See

[1]   Point Abino, the last Canadian cape before the entrance to Buffalo harbor, is a famous guide to mariners. It was near here that the *Walk-in-the-Water*, first steamship on the lakes, went down in 1821. Nearby is Crystal Beach Amusement Park, one of the biggest and liveliest on the Erie shore. Open summers.

[2]   The Niagara Parkway follows the river from lake to lake, from Fort Erie to Niagara-on-the-Lake. An outstanding scenic drive, it is lined with impressive waterfront homes, historic markers, and parks.

[3]   Overlooking the upper rapids of Niagara Falls is the palatial estate known as Oak Hall, built by mining magnate Sir Harry Oakes in 1928. The thirty-five-room mansion has been restored by the Parks Commission and five rooms are fitted with Oakes family treasures. Open late May to Labor Day, between 11:00 and 6:00. Below the home is Dufferin Islands Park, with paddleboats available to explore the recreation facility.

[4]   The block-long stretch of Clifton Hill is a surviving remnant of the honky-tonk spirit that once pervaded the falls area. If you want to sample just one of the attractions, try the Houdini Museum of Magic. It actually contains some interesting exhibitions on the art of illusionism and material used by the great escape artist himself in his performances. There is an admission fee. The rest of the attractions in the area lean heavily toward the ghoulish, the macabre, and the silly.

[5]   Three international bridges cross the river in the Niagara Falls area. Rainbow Bridge is in the vicinity of the falls. About one mile north is the Whirlpool Rapids Bridge, near the business district of Niagara Falls, Ontario. The newest bridge, near Queenston, connects the freeway bypasses around the area. All are toll bridges.

[6]   Just as impressive in its own right as the falls is the giant whirlpool formed by the river as it enters the narrow Niagara Gorge, two miles downstream. Most of the tightrope acrobats of the nineteenth century performed their stunts in this area. The Spanish Aero Cars give you some idea of what they saw from their precarious position. The cablecars take an 1,800-

foot long trip right above the furious whirlpool. The basin below contains sixty acres of enraged water, churned into an over-powering torrent as it enters the steep gorge. The Aero Cars operate from mid-April to mid-October; admission is charged.

[7]   Want to get even closer to the whirlpool? Take the Great Gorge Trip which brings you right down to water level by elevator. There is also an exhibit of the contrivances in which various zanies (here they are referred to as daredevils) have attempted to run the falls and whirlpool. Open April to October; admission charge.

[8]   The Niagara Glen, a bit to the north of the whirlpool, offers the more serious hiker an opportunity for a more strenu-ous excursion. Paths lead from the top of the bluffs to the river's edge. The park is operated by the Niagara Parks Commission.

[9]   All those floral displays throughout the Niagara parks did not get there by accident. The Parks Commission operates a school of horticulture and its grounds and gardens are open to visitors. It is just off the Niagara Parkway between the whirlpool and Queenston. The floral displays on its grounds are the result of class projects. There is no admission charge and it is open daily.

[10]   After American forces captured Fort George in 1813, they began making plans for the next move of the invasion. Laura Secord, a young woman who had troops billeted in her home near Queenston, overheard the discussions and trudged miles through the dark wilderness to warn the British command. The result was an American defeat at Beaver Dams and a sweet corner in Canadian history for Mrs. Secord. One of the country's top candy companies is named for her. The firm restored her home in Queenston and furnished it in the manner of an early nineteenth-cenury frontier homestead. Open mid-May to mid-October.

[11]   On the American side of the Niagara river, West River Parkway on Grand Island is a less photogenic version of the Canadian Niagara Parkway. Near its northern intersection with Interstate 190 is a view of Navy Island. Now a quiet 350-acre park, the island was once the focus of an international incident. William Mackenzie set up a base here after his abor-

tive revolt in Toronto was squashed in 1837. A supply ship sent to him by the United States was captured by the Canadians, a series of border incidents followed and for a time it seemed that war was imminent. But Mackenzie finally was jailed by the Americans in 1838, ending the affair. He later returned to Toronto where he spent the last twelve years of his life.

[12]   Niagara Falls, New York, is a much larger, more industrialized city than its Canadian counterpart. It has sightseeing attractions of its own, though. Principally, there is the marine aquarium, complete with performing electric eels. It is located on Whirlpool and Pine streets, a few blocks north and east of the Rainbow Bridge. Open daily; 9:00 to 7:00 in summer; 9:00 to 5:00 at other times; admission charge.

[13]   Rainbow Mall is the centerpiece of the rebuilt downtown of Niagara Falls. Besides its enclosed shopping facilities, it contains the Wintergarden, a conservatory of 7,000 tropical plants in a setting of pools and waterfalls. Also attached to the complex is the Native American Center for the Living Arts, an historical and art museum of the Indian cultures of the continent. It is housed in a building called The Turtle, named for its distinctive shape. It is open daily in summer, 10:00 to 8:00; closed Monday and Tuesday in winter with hours shortened to 10:00 to 5:00. There is an admission charge. The entire complex is located just south of the Rainbow Bridge plaza.

[14]   The Schoelkopf Museum, part of the Prospect Park area, explains Niagara's geologic aspects with displays and films. It is named for the family that founded the first hydroelectric company on the American side. It is open from Memorial Day to Labor Day, from 10:00 to 8:00; admission charge. The rest of the year it is open from 10:00 to 6:00; free. From November 2 to April 1, the museum is open Wednesday through Sunday only.

[15]   There's a fine view of the whirlpool from a state park along the Robert Moses Parkway, north of Niagara Falls. A mile farther north is Devil's Hole, a stretch of the Niagara Gorge named for an Indian massacre during Pontiac's Rebellion of 1763. A supply train and a relief column sent out from Fort Niagara were annihilated on the site.

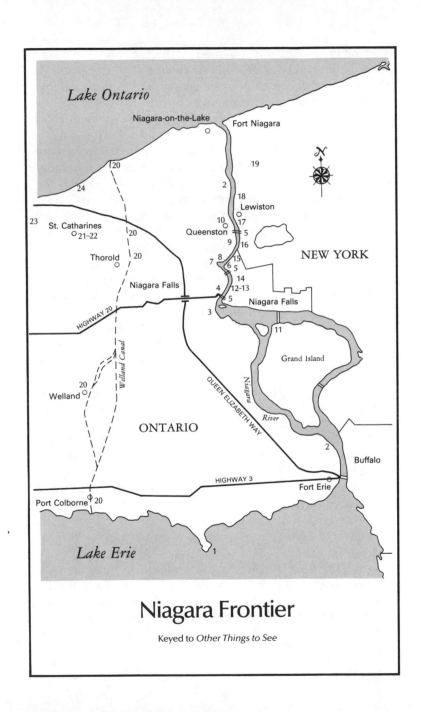

Niagara Frontier

Keyed to *Other Things to See*

HAMILTON

N

Lake Ontario

Hamilton Harbour

31

30

QUEEN ELIZABETH WAY

YORK ST.

29

BURLINGTON ST.

HIGHWAY 403

27

WELLINGTON ST.

28

JAMES ST.

KING ST.

QUEEN ST.

BAY ST.

26

MAIN ST.

MOUNTAIN PARK AVE.

HIGHWAY 20

25

MOHAWK RD.

[16]   The Power Vista, off the Moses Parkway, has awe-some views of the massive, three-quarter of a billion dollar power projects along the river. There is also an overlook back into the Gorge and historical displays. Open daily; free.

[**17**]   There is poetry tacked on the walls at the entrance, craftsmen and artists at work on the stairways, mime theater and concerts going on among the trees. This is Artpark, a cultural free-for-all in a 172-acre state park near the town of Lewiston, New York, along the river. There are workshops scheduled throughout the day, concerts and films going on periodically, and an air of awakening curiosity on every hand. A unique and arresting stop, especially if you are traveling with children. Open daily all year; charge for parking and for special events.

[18]   Lewiston itself is a graceful old town. Interesting shops line Center Street and several buildings date from the earliest years of the nineteenth century. James Fenimore Cooper spent some time here and gave a local setting to his revolutionary-era novel *The Spy*.

[19]   A fifteen-acre outdoor cathedral with fifty statues of the saints and a central dome makes up our Lady of Fatima Shrine. It is located between Lewiston and Youngstown, east of New York highway 18. Open daily; free.

[20]   The Welland Canal cuts across the middle of the Niagara Peninsula, from St. Catharines to Port Colborne. There are several places along its length where it is possible to ob-serve the lake freighters as they pass through the canal's locks and to get a feel for the heritage of this monumental engineer-ing feat that sends the commerce of the Great Lakes around the formidable detour of Niagara Falls.

In St. Catharines itself, visit the Historical Museum, featur-ing dioramas and displays relating to the construction and his-tory of the canal. You can also pick up a brochure there for a self-guided walk through the older section of the city. The museum is open weekdays, 9:00 to 5:00; weekends, 1:00 to 5:00. There is an admission charge.

There is a viewing platform at Lock Three, just south of the Queen Elizabeth Way overpass of the canal. An information office there posts anticipated arrival times for the freighters, so you can return later if you miss one the first time out.

The canal crawls over the Niagara Escarpment at the town of Thorold, and the Flight Locks there also provide viewing areas. Exit the Queen Elizabeth Way at Pine Street, turn north, and then east on Sullivan. The Lock Seven Motel features rooms with balconies overlooking the Flight Locks.

Until a bypass was constructed, the canal went right through the heart of Welland. Now the former route of the canal has been turned into a recreational waterway with adjacent parkland through the entire length of town, while a highway tunnels under the new canal east of town. Welland is also noted for its roses and a permanent rose display is at Chippewa Park.

Port Colborne is the Lake Erie outlet of the canal and Lock Eight there is among the longest locks in the world. Drive along West Street, south of the Clarence Street bridge, for a close-up view of the freighters. The park on the east bank of the canal also affords good opportunities for observing the nautical scene.

[21] St. Catharines sits in the midst of Ontario's greatest fruit belt. One of those fruits is the grape, which also makes the city the center of Canada's enological studies. Barnes Winery, the oldest in the country (1873) and Jordan Wines, one of Canada's largest, both offer tours most of the year. They are located west of the city and south of the Queen Elizabeth Way (Q.E.W.). Barnes is on Martindale Road, Jordan is on Louth. The city holds a wine festival each September.

[22] Another of St. Catharines's pleasant products is flower seeds. Stokes, the largest mail order seed house in Canada, opens its test garden to the public and it is a wondrous sight, an explosion of color. It is on Martindale Road, just north of the Queen Elizabeth Way (Q.E.W.); free.

[23] Lovely drives through the fruit belt can be made from St. Catharines by following the highway signs marked with a blossom along the Niagara escarpment. A series of roads follows the ridge from Queenston to Hamilton. One pleasant excursion leads to Ball's Falls Conservation Area, where a grist mill from the early nineteenth century still grinds. The best time to visit the area is blossom time, in early May.

[24]   St. Catharines is also big on rowing. Its Henley Regatta Course is regarded as the best of its kind on the continent.
It is in Port Dalhousie, a part of the city that once was a canal
town at the outlet of the third Welland Canal. (The current
route of the canal is the fourth one it has followed over the
years.) The Royal Canadian Regatta, second only to England's
Henley in age and importance, is usually held the first weekend
in August on the Henley Course.

[25]   In the summer of 1813, American forces made their
most serious effort to turn the Ontario lakehead and drive north
to Georgian Bay, thus splitting Ontario in half. They were
stopped at Stoney Creek, just east of Hamilton, by a surprise
British assault that succeeded in capturing two generals and
driving the Americans back to Niagara. A home that sits on the
battlefield, built in 1795, is now preserved as a museum of the
war period, with displays relating to Stoney Creek. The house is
open daily, 11:00 to 5:00, July 1 to Labor Day; daily 1:00 to
4:00, from Labor Day until mid-October; Sunday only, 1:00 to
4:00, the rest of the year. There is an admission charge. The
adjacent battlefield park is open daily all year, with no admission charge.

[26]   The views from the escarpment to the east of Hamilton are especially nice; so is the lookout over the central city
from Lawrence Park at the head of Wellington Street.

[27]   Hamilton may be a lunch-bucket steel town but the
fruit belt is right at its backdoor. The Farmer's Market, on
Merrick Street near North James Street, is the largest open-air
market in Canada and a reminder of the bounty a few miles
from the steel mills. It is held every Tuesday, Thursday, and
Saturday.

[28]   The downtown area of Hamilton has undergone a
radical change in recent years. Jackson Square, just behind the
market, with its office tower and enclosed mall, is one aspect of
the new look. So is the performing arts center at Hamilton
Place, the Art Gallery of Hamilton at 123 King Street West, and
the grouping of civic buildings between James and Bay Streets
and south of King Street, which includes parks, fountains, and
the Canadian professional football museum. The Gallery is

open Tuesday through Saturday, 10:00 to 5:00; Sunday, 1:00 to 5:00. There is no admission charge. The Football Hall of Fame is open weekdays, 10:00 to 4:00; weekends, 1:00 to 4:00. Closed Sunday from late November to late May. There is an admission charge.

[29]   A few blocks west of downtown Hamilton is Hess Village, a boutique and restaurant area in one of the city's graceful older neighborhoods on Hess Street at George.

[30]   Allan McNab, military hero and government leader, built his home on Burlington Heights, above the Hamilton harbor. Home is actually an understatement. Dundurn Castle, the largest restored nineteenth-century mansion in Canada, is open 10:00 to 5:00 in the summer; 1:00 to 4:00 the rest of the year. There is an admission charge.

[**31**]   The Royal Botanical Gardens occupies 2,000 acres just east of Hamilton. Star attraction is the rock garden, a flowering gem reclaimed from an abandoned gravel pit. Other notable displays are in the Laking Garden (herbaceous perennials), the Spring Garden, with its famous June lily displays, and the Rose Garden. Open daily, all year, daylight hours; no admission charge.

Side Trips

Lockport, New York, was built around a lock of the Erie Canal, and its Niagara County Historical Center preserves relics of pioneer days. It is open Wednesday to Friday, 10:00 to 5:00; weekends, 1:00 to 5:00. There is no admission charge. It is 21 miles east of Niagara Falls on New York 31.

In Wentworth Pioneer Village, thirty-three early nineteenth-century buildings from southern Ontario have been assembled to illustrate the development of a typical town of that era. Craft demonstrations are given throughout the day. It is located on Ontario 52, near Rockton, about 10 miles northwest of Hamilton. It is open every day but Monday, 10:00 to 5:00, mid-April to December 31. There is an admission charge.

Brantford, Ontario, was settled by members of the Six Nations tribes, who fought with the British in the Revolution, and was named for their chief, Joseph Brant. There is a historical museum in town, and on the outskirts is the lovely Chapel of the Mohawks, the oldest Protestant church in Ontario. It dates from 1782. The chapel is open daily, 10:00 to 6:00, in July and August; weekends only, 1:00 to 5:00, in April, May, September, and October. There is no admission charge. Another Brantford resident was Alexander Graham Bell. He conceived the idea that led to the invention of the telephone while home for a visit. The Bell Homestead is 5 miles southwest of town, off Highway 24. It is open daily, 10:00 to 6:00, mid-June to Labor Day. Closed Monday the rest of the year. There is no admission charge. Brantford is 25 miles west of Hamilton on Highway 2.

Kitchener is Canada's most Germanic city. Before World War I, in fact, it was called Berlin. The name was changed but each autumn it continues to hold an Octoberfest. Large groups of Mennonites also settled in the area and their farmer's market, featuring unique craft items and foods, is held every Wednesday and Saturday morning, June to mid-October. Prime Minister Mackenzie King was born in Kitchener, and his home, Woodside, is now a national historic park. The house is open daily, 10:00 to 5:00, all year. There is no admission charge. Kitchener, Ontario, is 35 miles northwest of Hamilton on Highway 8.

Parks on Lake Ontario and the Niagara River

Beaver Island—13 miles from Buffalo, New York, on the southern end of Grand Island. Beach, cafe, golf course. No camping.

Buckhorn Island—6 miles south of Niagara Falls, New York, on the northern end of Grand Island. Buckhorn Island is a wildlife sanctuary.

Four Mile Creek—15 miles north of Niagara Falls. Picnic grounds, 164 campsites.

Golden Hill—30 miles northeast of Niagara Falls. Picnic grounds, 38 campsites.

Reservoir State Park—4 miles northeast of Niagara Falls. Picnic grounds.

Whirlpool State Park—3 miles north of Niagara Falls, and

Devil's Hole, 4 miles north of Niagara Falls, have picnicking facilities. There is no swimming or camping at either of these parks.

The Niagara Parks Commission of Ontario operates two parks with campsites. Miller's Creek is 14 miles south of Niagara Falls on the Niagara Parkway. There is swimming nearby. Miller's Creek has 40 campsites. Charles Daley Park is 6 miles west of St. Catharines on the Queen Elizabeth Way (Q.E.W.). It has a Lake Ontario beachfront and refreshment stand. Charles Daley Park has 37 campsites.

If you go for a weekend: Stay in Niagara Falls, Ontario.

1. See the falls by any of the various methods outlined in this chapter.

2. Drive along the Niagara Parkway to Niagara-on-the-Lake, with a stop at the Gorge. Visit Queenston Heights along the way and take in a performance at the Shaw Festival, too.

3. Cross the river to New York and spend the morning at Fort Niagara. Visit Artpark in the afternoon, near Lewiston.

If you go for a week: Stay in Niagara Falls for four nights and Hamilton for three nights.

1–3. Same as the weekend tour.

4. Stroll Clifton Hill, Maple Leaf Village, and the other attractions of the Niagara Falls amusement area. Drive the southern half of the Niagara Parkway to Fort Erie.

5. Inspect the Welland Canal at the viewpoints at the Queen Elizabeth Way and the Thorold Lock. Continue on to Hamilton and walk through the city's central area.

6. On a day when the Farmer's Market is operating, take the side trip to Kitchener.

7. Visit the Royal Botanical Garden and take the side trip to Brantford to see the Bell Homestead and the Mohawk Chapel.

The slender needle of the Canadian National Tower soars 1,815 feet over Toronto.

2

Toronto

It was not too many years ago that Toronto would have finished very strong in the balloting for the dullest city in North America. It was a grey, stodgy old place with little tourist appeal.

Its Sunday closing laws were a national joke. Its frumpy image contrasted horribly with its sleek, chic rival Montreal, which never missed a chance to laugh down its nose at Toronto.

But nobody's laughing now. Within the span of a single generation, Toronto has transformed itself into one of the most exciting places anywhere. Its new skyline rises from the Lake Ontario shore, sending out the message that here the urban ideal still thrives. Thousands of Americans, residents of cities that are being torn apart by crime and suburban flight, flock here each weekend to walk the secure streets and rejoice in a good urban life they can no longer seem to find at home.

Toronto has managed to retain its heritage, too; preserving the best of it and blending the past with the contemporary. One of its most appealing areas is Yorkville, a district with roots firmly embedded in circa 1885.

A serviceman returning home to Toronto at the end of World War II would not have seen much difference from the town in which he had grown up. But the forces of change were bubbling just below the surface. Immigration from southern and eastern Europe already had begun. Canada was about to enter an economic boom that would concentrate unparalleled financial power in Toronto. A plan for metropolitan government, which had lain dormant since the 1920s, was about to be implemented.

If that soldier would gasp at the changes he would see in the next few years, one of the city's founders looking at the same transformation would have been utterly dumbfounded. This was not the type of place that Toronto's fathers—who called it York—had envisioned at all. The city was started by Governor-General John Graves Simcoe and an intrepid band of Loyalists in 1793 on the site of an old French trading post. Simcoe felt that Newark (now Niagara-on-the-Lake), then the capital of Upper Canada, was too exposed to American attack and wanted a more secure seat of government. York was burned nonetheless by American raiders in 1813 and the government buildings destroyed. The wartime experience only deepened the Loyalist distrust of the American democracy and its political and social institutions. These men had resisted the Revolution and remained loyal to the crown because of their opposition to any breath of egalitarianism. The government they developed in Upper Canada reflected these beliefs.

It was governed by an oligarchy, a tight combination of aristocratic families, Anglican clergy, and government officials known as the Family Compact. By 1834, when York officially became Toronto, rising immigration of Scotch and Irish laborers was creating a strong undercurrent of resentment. The discontent was fueled by William Lyon Mackenzie and his fire-breathing newspaper, the *Colonial Advocate*. It was a wild-swinging sheet that took on the Family Compact on every page. This firebrand was elected mayor in the same year the city's name was changed.

Mackenzie wanted to change more than a name. Frustrated as an elected official, he began preaching open rebellion. An army of about 700 of his followers, drawn primarily from the countryside, began marching down Yonge Street on December 5, 1837. A small band of citizens dispersed them with a volley of musket fire and the next day regular troops arrived. That ended the rebellion. Mackenzie fled to Navy Island in the Niagara River, almost touched off a war, and was finally jailed in America. He eventually returned to Toronto and lived quietly in a house on Bond Street.

After this moment of madness, Toronto settled down to more than a century of solid Tory prosperity. It became a great railhead and financial center. Literary visitors stopped there and wrote articles about how dull the place was. Its residents agreed with satisfaction. The most exciting thing that happened there was the fire of 1904 which wiped out much of the city's center.

Then the lid came off. The postwar boom brought money and power into the hands of new men, immigrants from other parts of Canada, and recently arrived refugees from Europe. Metro government went into effect in 1953. (Toronto is actually six municipalities—the central city plus York, North York, East York, Etobicoke, and Scarborough.) Construction activity was frenetic. New towers went up, not only downtown but all along the new subway lines and around the belt of freeways that cut through the outskirts of the city. Construction was taking place everywhere; new parks on the lake, a new city hall that is an architectural showcase, new underground shopping centers, new boutiques on staid Victorian streets. Even stern old Yonge Street developed a strip of enterprises dedicated to pleasures of the flesh (and even more esoteric delights). The Canadian National Tower, the most striking addition to the skyline, opened in 1976. A new crop of luxury hotels seemed to sprout every year.

Most visitors compare it to London, which is only natural considering its background. Like London, Toronto is a city of neighborhoods, several clusters of activity rather than one central business district. It has retained much of its intimate scale, too. The planners who at one time seemed determined to package the city into efficiently logical sterility apparently have been beaten off, and Toronto remains a place in which the human element is not dwarfed.

Some critics have complained that Toronto is such an eclectic place, borrowing so much from so many other cities, that it has no soul that is truly its own. Every visitor has to decide that for himself. If Toronto has borrowed, though, it borrowed only the best.

A Walk in Downtown Toronto

Toronto is a city that believes in getting the most out of its city halls. It turned its first one into a farmer's market when the city government moved out; it made the present one a showplace and the city's great public assembly point. A walk between the two buildings will take you from the historic heart of Toronto, through the central business district to some of the city's best attractions.

Start the stroll at the corner of Jarvis and Front Street East, three blocks east of Yonge Street. There are two buildings at the intersection that comprise the St. Lawrence Market. The flat, utilitarian structure on the north side of Front Street is not the one we are interested in. It was built in 1969 and is used as a market only on busy Saturdays. The ancient stone building on the south side of the street is our goal. It dates from 1844 and was Toronto's first city hall. Its occupants were somewhat less than pleased with it, though. "It was unfortunate for the reputation of the architect that he had not left the province before he completed the building, instead of afterward," wrote one contemporary critic. Extensive renovation work has made it hard to see what all the furor was about. The city did manage to put up with it for forty-six years before heading for new quarters. And the market, which had been located across the street, moved into the abandoned civic building. It is still there today and a colorful spectacle it is.

After inspecting the market's booths and stalls, walk one block north on Jarvis Street. On your left is Toronto's best preserved landmark from its past. This is St. Lawrence Hall, restored to its high Victorian luster during Canada's 1967 centennial. This lovely stone structure, complete with cupola, was built in 1850 and became the city's great meetinghall and auditorium for the balance of the century. The greatest performers and politicians of the age appeared here at one time or another. But as activity shifted to the west, the hall was deserted, later becoming an armory and eventually a flophouse. Ask the guard in the lobby for directions to the Great Hall; it has been restored to the elegance of its gas-lit prime. Closed Monday and Tuesday. There is no admission charge.

The replica of the English Gothic cathedral, just ahead of you on King Street as you leave the hall, is St. James Cathedral. It was built in 1853 quite deliberately on the model of a fourteenth-century cathedral. Set off as it is in a spacious park, much like a miniature close, the yellow-brick church carries off its medieval mission quite nicely. The steeple, completed twenty years after the rest of the church, is the tallest in Canada at 324 feet. For years the illuminated spire was the most distinctive part of Toronto's skyline and was used by ships as a navigation aid. Now it is a paltry new skyscraper indeed that does not soar twice as high as the old steeple.

Walk south on Church Street for one block to its intersection with Front and Wellington streets. The building occupying the triangle at which the three streets meet is the Gooderham Building, unavoidably known as the Flatiron Building. It was constructed in 1892 as an office for a distillery. The vantage point from the little park in front of it looking west toward downtown is a favorite with photographers. A picture of the curious old building, backed by the newly risen towers of the city behind it, appears at least twice a year in some Toronto newspaper.

The whole area east of Yonge Street is full of warehouses and offices erected in the late nineteenth century that are being put to contemporary use. Look especially at the row of grim, forbidding structures on the north side of The Esplanade, converted now into cheery restaurants and sidewalks cafes. Children will especially enjoy The Organ Grinder restaurant in this area. These conversions typify the preservationist philosophy that has turned Toronto into one of the most livable cities on the continent. Heading west on Front Street you will pass Toronto's compact theater district. St. Lawrence Centre for the Performing Arts was another centennial project, a civic successor to the old St. Lawrence Hall. There is a theater, with a repertory company in residence during the winter months, and a town hall inside. Right next door is the O'Keefe Centre, built by the brewing firm in 1960 and presented to the city as a gift. Its hall seats over 3,000 and is the scene of opera, ballet, and performances of visiting Broadway shows. The remainder of the

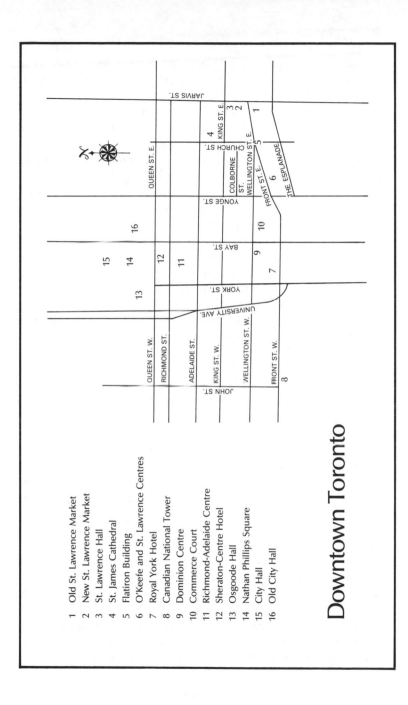

1   Old St. Lawrence Market
2   New St. Lawrence Market
3   St. Lawrence Hall
4   St. James Cathedral
5   Flatiron Building
6   O'Keefe and St. Lawrence Centres
7   Royal York Hotel
8   Canadian National Tower
9   Dominion Centre
10 Commerce Court
11 Richmond-Adelaide Centre
12 Sheraton-Centre Hotel
13 Osgoode Hall
14 Nathan Phillips Square
15 City Hall
16 Old City Hall

Downtown Toronto

intersection at Front and Yonge streets is made up of more vintage offices, including the Custom House (1876) and the Bank of Montreal (1885).

One block farther along Front Street will bring you to the grande dame of Toronto's hotels and a landmark in its own right, the Royal York. At its construction it was billed as the largest hotel in the British Empire. It remains a vast operation with 1,500 rooms but manages to achieve a level of personalized service that is the envy of hotels a quarter of its size. If it is mealtime or a sudden thirst strikes, there is ample occasion for relief in its fourteen restaurants and bars.

By now the slender needle of the Canadian National Tower will be right in front of you. It is hard to miss Toronto's answer to the Eiffel Tower. The structure stands 1,815 feet high and its observation platform, at the 1,465-foot mark, is billed as the highest such public facility in the world. There are restaurants and shopping in the base but the view is the thing here. It was said that one could see the spray from Niagara Falls from atop Toronto's tallest buildings. From this viewpoint you not only can see the spray but probably make out some of the rocks at the base and also what's for dinner in Buffalo. At night the lights of Rochester sometimes are visible across the lake. The harbor and islands on one side and the sprawling expanse of Metro Toronto on the other do make for a satisfying spectacle. There is also a revolving restaurant (Top of Toronto) on the lower observation level and a free multimedia show about the tower. Admission to the record-holding upper lookout deck involves another elevator ride and an added charge. Open daily, 9:00 A.M. to midnight.

Retrace your steps along Front Street, taking care to return to ground level before you do, all the way back to York Street, head north one block to Wellington Street and then east again. This brings you to Toronto Dominion Centre, first of the downtown superdevelopments. It opened in 1968. Mies Van der Rohe was the architect and was on hand as consultant during the construction process. Toronto Dominion Centre consists of three office towers, the highest at fifty-six stories, and a single-level pavilion. More than 18,000 people work in the complex.

Right across Bay Street is Commerce Court, opened five years after Toronto Dominion Centre. This project, containing the highest stainless steel office tower in the world, also retained and modernized the original skyscraper on the site, built in 1931. Its gargoyles, peering out over the city at the 300-foot level, symbolize, according to Commerce Court, "the eternal vigilance of the financier."

Chief attraction in both these complexes is the underground shopping malls. Toronto is slowly linking up an entire series of underground malls—much as Montreal has done—so that on blustery winter days shoppers can journey through the entire area and never so much as get a snowflake on their galoshes. Two other such malls are in operation a few blocks to the northwest—below the Richmond-Adelaide Centre and the Sheraton-Centre Hotel. You can make your way toward them by walking a block north on Bay Street to Adelaide Street and then turning left.

After your subterranean explorations, leave the Sheraton-Centre Hotel from the western or York Street exit and cross Queen Street to the north. Right in front of you is Osgoode Hall, another of Toronto's venerable treasures, headquarters for the Law Society of Upper Canada. The gates were originally intended to keep cows off the premises (this area was still pretty bucolic when construction began in 1829) but people are welcome. Take a look at the rotunda and staircase and, by permission of the librarian, the magnificent Great Library.

Across a driveway at the eastern end of the building lies Nathan Phillips Square and the new City Hall. This is a place to linger, for hours if you feel the inclination. On sunny days it seems that all of Toronto passes through this vast square, named after the mayor who instigated the civic construction program. The reflecting pool, walled in by lunchtime picnickers and sun seekers, becomes a skating rink in the winter. During the summer months, concerts and shows are put on in the square during the afternoons. If you are in town during the Canadian National Exhibition you will almost certainly encounter a tartan-clad brigade of pipers in the vicinity.

Across Bay Street is the Victorian pile of the old City Hall,

Toronto's second seat of urban government and the one that replaced the building at St. Lawrence Market. You may have noticed its clock tower, which closes off northbound Bay Street as you walked up from the Toronto Dominion Centre. This building, which was in service from 1890 to 1965, now houses a few law courts. There is some nice stained glass in the main lobby and the carillon chimes the hours for the edification of those basking in the sun in the square across the street.

Elevated walkways enable you to get another perspective on the human panorama in the huge square. In the northwest corner is Henry Moore's sculpture, *The Archer,* acquired in 1969 through public subscription. It aroused some controversy at the time, but not nearly as much as did the City Hall itself.

Just like the first City Hall more than a century before, this striking complex also had its detractors. Even now Torontonians affectionately refer to it as "the clam." The architect was Finnish designer Viljo Revell, who won an international competition for the assignment. He died the year before his masterwork was finished, never knowing that his critics would be snuffed out by popular acclamation. In this case the people voted with their seats and as they perch here every afternoon they reaffirm the success of Revell's concept more decisively than any panel of architectural experts. Tours of the facility are given every half hour on weekdays, 10:15 to 5:45; free.

Yorkville

Toronto seems to show its sunniest face to visitors in Yorkville. Many weekend drop-ins never leave the few square blocks that define its limits, a mile or so north of downtown. They stay in its hotels, eat in its restaurants, shop in its boutiques and endlessly stroll its streets. The three-block stretch of Bloor Street between Yonge Street and Avenue Road is the main promenade. But the side streets north of Bloor have their allure, too. It is a fascinating urban area, the very essence of gracious city living to many minds. It also typifies what has happened to Toronto over the last generation or so.

Yorkville started out as a separate village, the first way station north out of York on the long road up to Lake Simcoe. The larger city to the south swallowed up the former village in 1883 and it became a pleasantly nondescript sort of neighborhood for the next half century or so. Some signs of decay even had set in by the end of World War II.

In the middle 1950s, though, a few artists discovered a certain charm in the old Victorian neighborhood and, attracted by the cheap rents, they started opening up studios and galleries in the area. The serious artists were followed, as they usually are, by the pseudo-Bohemians, those who enjoy playing at art and poverty. Within a few years this group had developed into the hippie movement of the 60s. As the media discovered them, curious crowds began coming up for a look at these odd folk—much as they did in San Francisco's Haight-Ashbury and similar locales. In other cities the hippie district either turned brutal and crime-ridden or fizzled out in a drab heap of head shops and bookstores. In Toronto, though, it attracted a group of imaginative entrepreneurs who decided to hold on to the crowds by fashioning snazzy boutiques, expensive galleries, sidewalk cafes, and the like out of the material at hand. The hippies and others of that ilk have been priced out. Yorkville now comprises some of the most expensive real estate in the city. This is high-rise expense account territory today. But the area still retains its charm, even if the prices in its stores may exceed the girth of your bankroll.

A pleasant introductory walk in the Yorkville area starts a few blocks south on University Avenue. Take the subway to the Queen's Park exit and you will emerge, unsurprisingly, in Queen's Park, right in front of the impressive provincial Parliament buildings. The pink sandstone structures were constructed between 1886 and 1893 and in her proper place on the front lawn amid the flowers sits a statue of Queen Victoria. A few yards away from her statue is that of John A. Macdonald, Canada's first prime minister. There is a museum inside and tours of the chamber are available every half hour on weekdays during July and August. Hours vary when the legislature is in session so it is best to call in advance.

Across the western half of Queen's Park Crescent, the curving thoroughfare alongside the legislature, is the very pleasant Sigmund Samuel Museum of antique Canadiana. It features complete room settings of various periods and locations from Canada's past, including an 1820s wood-panelled room from Quebec that was reassembled here intact. Open 10:00 to 5:00, Monday through Saturday, 1:00 to 5:00, Sunday; free.

A few steps north from the museum will take you to the gateway of the University of Toronto. At least two of the buildings on the atmospheric campus are worth a look. On your right as you enter is the student center, Hart House, built with Oxford and Cambridge very much on its designers' minds. It dates from the World War I years. Seek out the Great Hall, the dining room, a bit of the old school if there ever was one. Next as you proceed along the university crescent is University Hall, regarded as the most distinguished building on campus. Built in 1859, in the Romanesque style popular then, its interior staircase leading to its two great halls is worth the climb.

Return through the university gate and cross Queen's Park Crescent for a short stroll through the park. The two halves of the crescent reunite in a little while and shortly thereafter on your left will be the museum complex of the McLaughlin Planetarium and Royal Ontario Museum (ROM). The ROM is a staggering collection, an overwhelming array of exhibits from the fields of archeology, geology, mineralogy, zoology, and paleontology, and the displays represent just a fraction of it all.

Yorkville

1   Ontario Parliament
2   Sigmund Samuel Museum
3   University of Toronto
4   Royal Ontario Museum
5   Hazelton Lanes
6   The Colonnade
7   Park Plaza Hotel
8   Windsor Arms Hotel

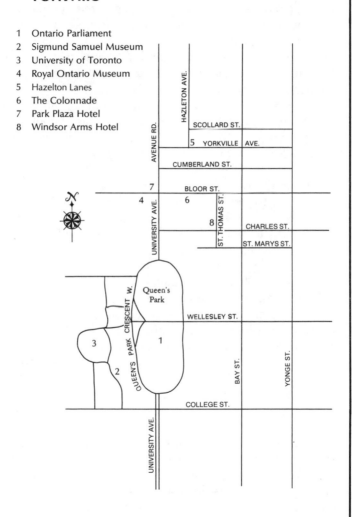

You should give at least one day to the museum and attached planetarium. But if you are in a hurry, the two *can't-miss* attractions are the dinosaur hall on the second floor, with room after room of terrible lizards displayed in their probable habitat; and the Chinese collections on the third floor, the most extensive and breathtaking in North America. The museum is open between 10:00 and 9:00, Tuesday through Saturday; 1:00 to 9:00 on Sunday and 10:00 to 5:00 on Monday. There is an admission charge.

Out the door of the ROM and a quick left takes you to Bloor Street and the beginning of Yorkville. Simply cross the street (observe that University Avenue changes its name to Avenue Road on the other side) and you are there. The area's most attractive asset is the sense of surprise and discovery that comes from wandering its streets. Yorkville is compact and lends itself to unhurried examination on foot. That's the best, really the only way, to see it. Other interesting streets to wander in addition to Bloor are Cumberland, Yorkville, and Scollard streets (which parallel Bloor on the north); Hazelton Avenue which runs north from Yorkville Avenue, and St. Thomas, a gracious block-long street running south from Bloor. Art galleries, import shops, clothing stores, craft outlets, intriguing bookstores— almost anything you have ever felt an impulse to buy can be found along these streets. Nearby, a few blocks to the north on Avenue Road and east along Davenport Road, there is another area of specialty shops that has opened in the last few years.

One of Yorkville's most distinctive features is the shopping court, a central, open plaza surrounded by several levels of shops. The entire area is honeycombed with such operations, and part of the fun is seeking them out. More seem to open every year. If it should rain, simply head for The Colonnade, an indoor version of the shopping court at 131 Bloor Street West. Its Cafe de la Paix is perfect for a snack. Or try Hazelton Lanes, which is even more representative of the new generation of elaborate indoor malls that have come into this area.

The Park Plaza on the northwest corner of Bloor and Avenue Road is Yorkville's traditional established hotel. Longtime Toronto residents like to gather at its rooftop bar for a nostalgic interlude. For those with a taste for the continental touch, the tiny Windsor Arms on St. Thomas Street is probably the best small hotel in Canada. Its equally minuscule dining area, the Three Small Rooms, is very popular, and right across the street is one of the city's finest French restaurants, Le Provencal. If that does not quite suit your fancy, just wander a bit more. The concentration of good restaurants in these few blocks is intense. There is no need for anyone to go hungry in Yorkville.

Ontario Place and the Toronto Islands

There are some Great Lakes cities that might just as well be on the Great Plains for all the use they make of their water. Their lakefront or riverfront has long since been usurped by railroads or highways or warehouses. One can travel for miles along the water without ever catching a glimpse of the lake through the warren of buildings. No parks, not even a patch of green, break the view.

There are, however, two notable exceptions. One is Chicago, the other is Toronto. The fact that they happen to be the two most appealing cities on the lakes is by no means coincidental.

Toronto has developed two facilities on its lakefront that are models of urban design. One, the remarkable Ontario Place, is a man-made, ninety-six-acre park. The other, the Toronto Islands, is a natural park developed with restraint and wisdom by the city. The two of them are as fine an example of waterfront land use as you are liable to find anywhere.

Ontario Place is modeled a little bit on Montreal's wildly acclaimed Expo '67 (many planners worked on both projects) and a little bit on Copenhagen's Tivoli Gardens. Its domes and towers rise like a candy kingdom from three islands adjacent to the Canadian National Exhibition grounds, west of downtown. It is, above all, a very attractive place. The views of the city skyline from its pavilions suspended out over the water of Lake Ontario are wonderful. The landscaping is done with care. There are lagoons to walk by and marinas to stroll past and a promenade along the lake.

But there is a tremendous sense of excitement, too, a feeling of thrilling things in progress or just about to happen. On a summer afternoon there is likely to be a steel band roving the premises, pounding out calypso rhythms and drawing children in its wake like a Caribbean Pied Piper. There are free shows in the Forum all summer long. During the afternoon you may wander past and see the National Ballet of Canada in rehearsal for the evening's performance of "Swan Lake." You can sit down and watch if you like. Hundreds do. There are also shows going on in the Cinesphere, the giant movie theater that resembles a huge golf ball from a distance. In the pods above the lake there are the Experiential Theatres, a series of mixed media shows. There is, above all, the sound of children having the time of their lives. Ontario Place sets aside two of its acres as the exclusive preserve of kids from ages four to fourteen. Children's Village is divided into two sections, Landplay and Waterplay, and the latter section is as moist as the name implies. Special driers take off the damp when the youngsters are ready to leave. Ontario Place also is loaded with restaurants of varied price range and ethnic bent and there are plenty of shops, as well. One admission covers all the attractions in the park. Open daily from late May to Labor Day, 10:30 to 1:00 A.M.; then weekends only until mid-October.

From the Ontario Place boat dock, cruises leave hourly each afternoon for the Toronto Islands. The cruises, operated by Simpson's Boat Tours, also may be boarded at the foot of Yonge Street. They are a pleasant introduction to the city's island parks. The best way to further your acquaintance is to take the ferryboat from the Yonge Street dock and explore on your own.

The islands are accessible only by boat (or by plane, if you have one, since there's an airstrip) and no motorized vehicles are permitted. So even though they are virtually in the shadow of Toronto's business district, the islands are a world away from the pace of the big city. However, they tend to get crowded on summer weekends and it is best to avoid the peak hours on the boats. Even bicycles are not permitted aboard then, so congested are the decks.

The islands once were connected to the mainland by a sandspit but have been marooned since 1857 when a violent storm severed that line. Three yacht clubs are based here, including the Royal Canadian which calls itself the largest freshwater yacht club in the world.

Centre Island is the major destination and it contains most of the park's formal attractions. There are canoe rentals, picnic groves, gardens, dancing, an old lighthouse, and a miniature working farm. A small amusement park, modeled on a rural Ontario settlement of the last century, called Centreville, operates from late May to Labor Day. The island even has two churches, one Anglican and one Catholic, which are very popular spots for weddings. If you are lucky you may share the boat ride over to the islands with the bridal party.

The other large island is Ward's (there are several smaller ones) and it is connected to Centre by a footbridge along Lakeshore Boulevard. Despite its impressive name, the boulevard is simply a narrow road. The ferry from the mainland also stops at Ward's and is almost always less crowded than the one to Centre Island. Ward's is much less developed and is a splendid getaway place, affording excellent views of the lake and a unique perspective on the Toronto skyline.

Other Things to See

[1]   Joseph Brant, a chief of the Six Nations, aided the British during the American Revolution. When the war was over, he and his displaced followers were compensated with land grants along Ontario's Grand River. Eventually, Brant built his own home, which he called Wellington Square, at the head of Lake Ontario. His landholdings became the city of Burlington and his home was rebuilt on its original site in 1939. It is now a museum of his life and the region. It is on North Shore Boulevard, just east of the Queen Elizabeth Way (Q.E.W.). Open Monday through Saturday, 10:00 to 5:00; Sunday, 1:00 to 5:00; admission charge.

[2]   The sights and sounds of an Ontario farming community of the nineteenth century are recreated in Black Creek Pioneer Village in North York on the northern border of Metro Toronto. Five buildings of the Stong Farm remain on their original sites and twenty-five others have been moved here from other parts of the province. There is a museum in a cantilever barn dating from 1809. The village is open daily, 10:00 to 6:00 in summer; 10:00 to 5:00 in spring and fall. It is closed from January 1 to mid-March. There is an admission charge.

[3]   Hockey Night in Canada is an institution on both sides of the border so it is fitting that the sport's Hall of Fame is in Toronto where the broadcasts originate. The collection of memorabilia and the famous Stanley Cup are on the grounds of the Canadian National Exhibition (CNE), west of downtown. The Hall is open daily, 10:00 to 8:00 in summer, 11:00 to 9:00 during the CNE, and Tuesday through Sunday, 10:00 to 4:30, the rest of the year. There is an admission charge.

[4]   Also on the CNE grounds is the Marine Museum of Upper Canada, tracing Toronto's part in the history of Great Lakes shipping to the days of the St. Lawrence Seaway. The restored steam tug *Ned Hanlan* is berthed nearby. Open 9:30 to 5:00; Sunday, noon to 5:00. There is an admission charge.

[5]   The CNE itself runs from mid-August to Labor Day and is one of the biggest fairs in the world. There's name entertain-

ment, corps of pipers, parades, pageantry, and the hoopla of an overgrown county fair. There is an admission charge.

[6]   When the invading American army landed at York in 1813, the retreating British garrison blew up the fort. The explosion killed the American second-in-command, Zebulon Pike, for whom Colorado's Pike's Peak was named. The Americans stayed a week, and Fort York was rebuilt upon their departure. It was restored in the 1930s but most of the eight remaining structures date from the earlier reconstruction. The Fort York Guard drills in the summer. Fort York is located west of downtown on the way to the CNE grounds, on Garrison Road at Fleet Street. Open daily; Sunday afternoon only, except in summer; admission charge.

[7]   What can be done with a waterfront dotted with obsolete marine terminals and aging warehouses? In Toronto's case, it can be turned into still another entertainment and shopping complex. That's how Harbourfront was born, the newest addition to the city's lakeshore scene. It is a dazzling row of indoor and outdoor facilities along the city's waterfront, between Yonge Street and Spadina Road. The former Marine Terminal, an Art Deco showcase, was the latest segment of the development to open in the summer of 1983. On summer evenings it seems that half of the city comes here to enjoy the waterfront.

[8]   Ed Mirvish, genial proprietor of Honest Ed's Discount Department Store, took over an entire block of decrepit houses on Markham Street in 1963 and turned it into his very own self-contained shopping mall, known as Markham Street Village. In addition to Mirvish's weird department store there are some antique shops, a few cozy restaurants, an ice cream store, two bookstores, and plenty of other shoppers and strollers to ogle. It is just south of Bloor Street, about one mile west of Yorkville.

[9]   Sir Henry Pellatt was an incurable romantic. Since he was also very wealthy he was able to indulge his medieval fantasies by building his own castle in the middle of Toronto in 1911. He just about went broke in the process and Casa Loma had to be taken over for taxes by the city. The ninety-eight-room castle, with its fantastic furnishings and unique architectural features, could hardly be duplicated at any price today.

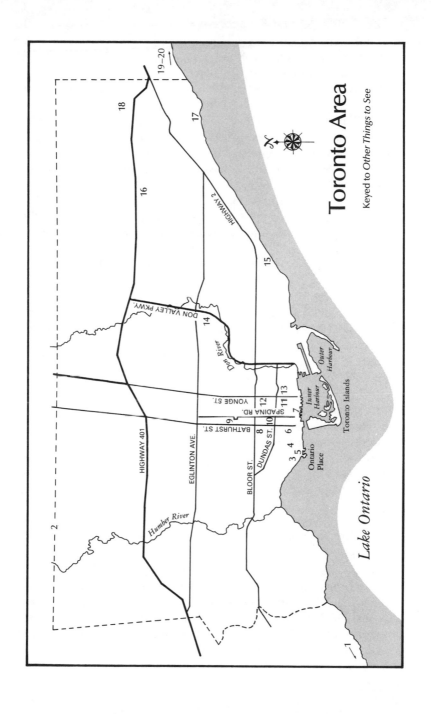

Toronto Area

Keyed to Other Things to See

Lake Ontario

Toronto Islands

Outer Harbour

Inner Harbour

Ontario Place

HIGHWAY 401

EGLINTON AVE.

DON VALLEY PKWY.

HIGHWAY 2

BLOOR ST.

BATHURST ST.

DUNDAS ST.

SPADINA RD.

YONGE ST.

Don River

Humber River

1
2
3
4
5
6
7
8
9
10
11
12
13
14
15
16
17
18
19–20

Located on Davenport Road at Spadina Road. Open daily, 10:00 to 4:00; admission charge.

[10]   Toronto's Kensington district is a polyglot section of the city and the center of activity is the European-style Kensington Market. It is perfect for shoppers who like to haggle and also great fun for those who only want to stand around and look. Surrounding streets abound in ethnic eating places. Located on Spadina Road, between College and Dundas streets, the market opens at 6:00 A.M. every day but Sunday.

[11]   The Henry Moore Sculpture Centre, containing 300 original works by the British artist, is the chief attraction of the Art Gallery of Ontario. There is also a large collection of Canadian artwork. The Grange, right behind the Gallery, is a Georgian mansion, the oldest brick house in Toronto, dating from 1817. It once housed the Art Gallery, but when the new structure was completed in 1974 the Grange was restored to its appearance of the 1835–40 era. The buildings are located on Dundas Street West, about four blocks west of the St. Patrick subway stop. Open 10:00 to 5:00, Monday through Saturday; until 10:00 on Wednesday and Thursday; 12:00 to 5:00 on Sunday. Donation asked.

[12]   The bawdy, gaudy Yonge Street Strip is one of the city's top areas for walking and looking. It runs south from Bloor Street. Midway between Bloor Street and downtown on Yonge is Eaton Centre, a gigantic indoor mall, occupying an entire city block, which has become the city's foremost shopping place. It is more like a complete indoor city, with every conceivable facility not only available but available in triplicate, at least. The main entrance is on Yonge at Dundas Street.

[13]   When radical journalist and politician William Lyon Mackenzie returned from his American exile in 1849 he reentered public life and served in the Legislative Assembly for nine years. When he retired his admirers bought him a home at 82 Bond Street and he spent the last three years of his life there. Restored in mid-nineteenth-century decor, the house is two blocks east of Yonge Street and just south of Dundas Street. Open Monday through Saturday, 9:30 to 5:00; Sunday, 12:00 to 5:00. There is an admission charge.

[**14**]   The visitor becomes part of the displays at the Ontario Science Centre, in which participation is encouraged in
order to make science a tangible experience. There are 550
exhibits and in most of them you are invited to get into the act.
Youngsters find the museum one of the most engrossing attrac-

Shops, restaurants, movies: multilevelled Eaton Centre has it all. *Photograph
by Doris Scharfenberg.*

tions in the city. It is northeast of downtown on Don Mills Road at Eglinton Avenue East. Open daily, 10:00 to 6:00; admission charge.

[15]   The Beach is a raffish sort of neighborhood, a resort appendage to the big city. It has boardwalks on the lakefront, plenty of parks, and an intriguing shopping strip along Queen Street East. The area runs east from Greenwood Avenue.

[16]   Unique city halls seem to be a Toronto tradition. The easternmost borough of Scarborough has one of the most sensible around. It combines not only the functions of government, but also places for public assembly and an enormous shopping center—kind of a regional all-in-one stop. Architect Raymond Moriyama developed the concept. It opened in 1973. Located just south of Highway 401 on McCowan Road. Daily tours every half hour, 10:00 to 6:00.

[17]   The Scarborough Bluffs, rising 300 feet above the lake shore in some places, can be viewed to good advantage from a park at the foot of Midland Avenue. But it is even more fun to look at the bluffs from the grounds of the Guild Inn. Built as a private residence atop the bluffs in 1914, it became a hotel twenty-four years later and is still serving that function, with a modern wing added on to the original. A cedar maze leads to the edge of the bluffs and there are fifty acres of grounds surrounding the old estate. It is located in far-flung Scarborough off Highway 2.

[18]   Metro Toronto Zoo, opened in 1974, presents animals grouped by geographic habitat on its 710 acres. Natural settings are emphasized and the parklike setting of the zoo itself is part of the appeal. It is on Meadowvale Road, just north of Highway 401. Open all year. Hours are from 10:00 to 7:00 in summer, 10:00 to 5:00 in spring and fall, 10:00 to 3:30 in winter. There is an admission charge and parking fee.

[19]   Oshawa is one of Canada's major automotive centers, headquarters of General Motors of Canada. It was the hometown of Robert S. McLaughlin, who joined his pioneer automotive firm to the American corporate giant and became president of the Canadian affiliate. McLaughlin died in 1972 and his twelve-acre estate Parkwood, with a fifty-five-room mansion and exten-

sive art collection, is in the northern part of town at 270 North Simcoe Street. Take the Simcoe Street exit from Highway 401. The home is open daily except Monday, June through August, 10:30 to 4:00. In May and September through November, Wednesday and Sunday only, 1:30 to 4:00. It is open the rest of the year but by appointment only.

[20]   Also in Oshawa, the history of the motorcar is traced from a Canadian perspective at the Canadian Automotive Museum, 99 Simcoe Street South. Open Monday through Saturday and Sunday afternoon; admission charge.

Side Trips

The McMichael Canadian Collection presents the works of artists, especially the Group of Seven, who broke away from British academic tradition around the turn of the century to found a style rooted in Canadian experience. The works are housed in a striking gallery of stone and hand-hewn timbers surrounded by forest. It is in Kleinburg, about 23 miles northwest of Toronto on Highway 27.

The Sharon Temple, built in 1825, is a singular three-story church erected by a pioneer religious sect, the Children of Peace. Now a museum, it is open every day but Tuesday, mid-May to mid-October. Sharon is about 33 miles north of Toronto, east from Highway 11.

Toronto Parks

Toronto is a city that knows how to use its green space. Two streams, the Humber and the Don, flow through the city and their banks are given over to parkland for most of the route. On a map, these parks show up as slender ribbons around the core of the city. In reality they look even nicer.

The Humber parks are mostly in Etobicoke, the western-most borough of Metro Toronto. Except for a few short gaps they run continuously from the northern Metro limits to Lake Ontario. Some of the more interesting points are James Gardens, formal gardens off Royal York Road on Edenbridge Drive; the wildflower gardens in adjoining Scarlett Mills Park; and the Old Mill, dating from 1849 and now a restaurant overlooking the valley. It is accessible from the subway stop of the same name.

High Park, just east of the Humber ribbon, is a 350-acre facility, a busy urban retreat which is closed to motorized traffic on weekends and holidays. Much of its central portion was donated to the city by architect John Howard. His home, Colborne Lodge, built in 1836, is open all year. Hours are Monday through Saturday, 9:30 to 5:00; Sunday, 12:00 to 5:00; admission charge.

Toronto Island parks—see pages 58–60.

The Central Don parks are the east side's equivalents of the Humber parks. They comprise seven miles of connected parkway along the river. Edwards Gardens, on Lawrence Avenue East at Leslie Street, is a thirty-five-acre hillside display, probably the most beautiful in the city. The three parks to the south— Wilket Creek, Serena Gundy, and Sunnybrook—have a full range of recreational facilities, including riding stables. The resort hotel, Inn on the Park, overlooks all the greenery and is a favorite of those seeking a rural atmosphere while remaining in the city. To the south of this area, Taylor Creek offers hiking in less developed surroundings.

There are swimming facilities in the Eastern Beaches Park on Lake Ontario. A narrow strip of beachfront park runs from the Humber parks to downtown, between the lake and the railroad tracks.

If you go for a weekend: Stay in Toronto.

1. Take the Yorkville walk outlined in this chapter.

2. Take the Downtown walk outlined in this chapter. If you plan to stay into the week, buy tickets now for a concert or play.

3. Visit the city's waterfront; Ontario Place, the Toronto Islands, and Harbourfront.

If you go for a week: Stay in Toronto the entire time.

1–3. Same as the weekend tour.

4. Spend a day at the Ontario Science Centre.

5. Drive out to Black Creek Pioneer Village in the morning,

then continue north on Highway 400 to Kleinburg and see the McMichael Collection.

6. Browse through one of the city's spectacular enclosed shopping malls, then to the zoo in the afternoon.

7. Visit Casa Loma, Fort York, and the Kensington Market. If the weather is good, go to one of the city's public beaches on Lake Ontario.

The graceful dome of City Hall dominates the harbor at Kingston, Ontario. *Courtesy Ontario Ministry of Industry and Tourism.*

Loyalist Country

3

The losers of the American Revolution are given widely different roles in the study of national history, depending on which side of the border you get your education. In America they are called Tories. There are a few words of regret over the harsh treatment afforded some of them by the victorious rebels and then the Tories disappear from the history books. In Canada, however, they are known as Loyalists, esteemed as valiant defenders of a losing cause, and they play an integral part in the development of the nation.

By some estimates more than half of the residents of colonial New York did not support the Revolution. Many of them took up arms for the crown. The lands west of Schenectady were among the bloodiest battlegrounds of the war, with Loyalist guerillas being a constant menace to the area. For these men, going home after the war was out of the question. Return would have probably meant death, or at least severe punishment. So out of necessity, and in many cases out of choice, they gave up their property and fortunes and headed across the frontier established by the Treaty of Paris to start life once more under British rule. One historian calls them the displaced persons of the eighteenth century, and that is not far from the mark.

A sizable contingent of Loyalists settled in Nova Scotia. Others moved to the Niagara Frontier. A third group settled along the St. Lawrence Valley and down the northern shore of Lake Ontario. Aside from the settlements at Kingston and around Niagara, this entire vast lakeside territory had been little more than wilderness until the aftermath of revolution brought these able newcomers into the region. It was by no means the majority of Loyalists who came here. Far more returned to England or opted for the softer climates of British possessions in the South Atlantic or Caribbean. Those who did settle around Lake Ontario, though, secured Canada for British rule and made possible its later independence. If the Loyalists had not made this a permanently settled country it is almost certain that Britain eventually would have been forced to turn over the whole territory to the United States, which attempted to win it by conquest anyhow in 1812.

The genuine Loyalists, who are properly called United Empire Loyalists, were joined in later years by other Americans, primarily New Englanders. They were attracted by free land rather than any great loyalty to the crown but they called themselves Loyalists just the same to be eligible for the giveaways. The northern lakeshore is still keenly aware of its Loyalist heritage. The word is seen often along the road here, frequently as part of the name of a business, much as Lone Star would be used in Texas. Nearly every town has a Loyalist shrine of some kind—a home, church, or museum.

The pattern of settlement on Lake Ontario is the mirror image of the way Lake Erie developed. Here it is the Canadian shore that is thickly settled and commercially developed, while the American lakefront, with the exception of Rochester, is mainly rural and sparsely populated. The Erie Canal drew American development away from the lake to its route. In Canada, though, the lake was the main highway of commerce and the prosperous cities grew up on the shore.

Kingston, situated in one of the continent's most strategic locations, the junction of the Great Lakes and the St. Lawrence River, is among the oldest settlements on the lakes. It began as the French Fort Frontenac in 1673 and grew into Montreal's trading outpost with the Indians of the West.

It was the base of Britain's Lake Ontario fleet during the War of 1812. Fort Henry was built nearby to guard its location at the mouth of the passage to eastern Canada's interior. By a natural process of evolution, Canada's Royal Military College was founded here in 1876 between the fort and the city. When Ontario and Quebec combined to form the Province of Canada in 1841, Kingston was named the capital. Its term as the nation's hub lasted only three years. The legislators preferred the more sophisticated attractions of Montreal and the capital was moved there in 1844. That touched off an economic depression in Kingston, resulting from overbuilding during its brief whirl with national power. Kingston had the last word, though. Its own member of Parliament, John A. Macdonald, became Canada's first prime minister when confederation was realized in 1867.

Highway 401 now shoots through this area on its nonstop way from Toronto to Montreal, and many travelers shoot right along with it. To Americans especially, Kingston is not nearly as well known as it should be. The smaller towns are hardly noticed at all. This is a fascinating corner of Canada to linger in, a bit different from the rest of the country. It is a land that still feels the hurt of a war lost 200 years ago.

A Walk through Kingston

Kingston is a city of stones and domes. It is called the Limestone City because of the wealth of stone buildings remaining from its great years of expansion in the 1840s. Because most of these stately buildings were erected when classical architecture was in vogue, the most striking feature of the city's skyline is its domes. From the ramparts of Fort Henry, the Frontenac County Courthouse, St. George's Cathedral, and City Hall can be picked out easily from the other city heights. The characteristic blue-grey tinge of the native limestone might be expected to give Kingston a rather somber tone. But that is not the case at all. Kingston's old stones usually are surrounded by flowers and set off by parks. Even the ancient stone penitentiary faces a marina and harbor which hosted the sailing events of the 1976 Olympic Games.

City Hall is the focus of activity. It faces the waterfront in the midst of Kingston's historic district. It is an impressive old building with its domed clock tower and pillars and masterful stonework. And well it should be. The city just about went broke building it. City Hall was planned when Kingston was named capital of Canada in 1841. It was decided that the seat of the national government should have a suitable home for its local government as well. By the time it was finished, though, the capital had decamped for Montreal and Kingston was in the midst of a depression. The city even offered to turn over its new City Hall to the government rent free if it would just stay put. Nothing doing. In desperation, Kingston scoured the city for any tenant willing to rent space in the handsome new edifice. For the next fifteen years, parts of City Hall were rented out to saloons, banks, a dry goods store, and even as apartments. But prosperity eventually returned, and the building was able to function, at last, as a city hall. It was restored to its original freshness in 1973. Tours of the interior are given at varying times throughout the year.

Confederation Park, a fountain-splashed piece of green adorned with an arch, lies between City Hall and the harbor. The Chamber of Commerce Tour Train leaves from the park

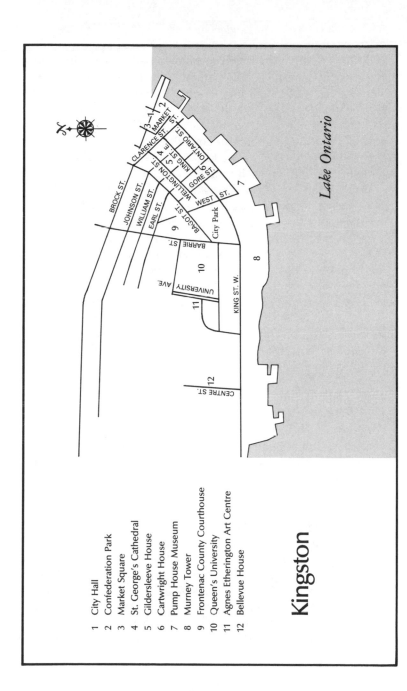

Lake Ontario

N

1 City Hall
2 Confederation Park
3 Market Square
4 St. George's Cathedral
5 Gildersleeve House
6 Cartwright House
7 Pump House Museum
8 Murney Tower
9 Frontenac County Courthouse
10 Queen's University
11 Agnes Etherington Art Centre
12 Bellevue House

Kingston

BROCK ST.
JOHNSON ST.
WILLIAM ST.
EARL ST.
WELLINGTON ST.
CLARENCE ST.
KING ST. E.
ONTARIO ST.
MARKET ST.
GORE ST.
WEST ST.
BAGOT ST.
BARRIE ST.
UNIVERSITY AVE.
KING ST. W.
CENTRE ST.
City Park

daily in July and August on a motorized, 10-mile trip around the city's major sights. The park also opens out on nice views over the head of Lake Ontario and of the ferryboat leaving for Wolfe Island at the mouth of the St. Lawrence River. The fountain and arch were built during the 1967 centennial year as a tribute to Kingston's role in confederation.

Behind City Hall is the Market Square. There was space set aside in the building itself for a market but the stalls now are set up outside on Tuesdays, Thursdays, and Saturdays. Walled in by some of the city's most venerable commercial establishments, the market makes a handsome scene. Some of the oldest structures on the square are the row of limestone buildings across Market Street. They date in part from 1817. The Customs House and the Post Office, both erected in the 1850s and typical of the use of limestone in the city's public buildings, lie one block away at the corner of Clarence and Wellington streets.

King Street, at the western end of the Market Square, is the street we want. The major thoroughfare in town, many of Kingston's most interesting buildings and neighborhoods lie along its length. One block down is the dome and clock tower of St. George's Anglican Cathedral. The building dates from 1825, although the dome, built in imitation of Sir Christopher Wren's London churches, was added as recently as 1891. The congregation was founded in 1792 and for the next seventy years Dr. John Stuart and his son, George, were the only clergymen the church ever had. It became a cathedral in 1862, the same year the younger Stuart died. The original building was a rectangle, but the King Street portico and clock tower were added in an 1840s enlargement, another benefit from the city's short term as capital. Lord Sydenham, who presided over the unification of Canada in 1840, is buried here. Banners of the Royal Military College cadets hang from their reserved balcony on the right. The cathedral choir has toured Europe, the first North American group to sing in Britain's great cathedrals.

Across Johnson Street is the Gildersleeve House, built in 1825 by one of the late-arriving Loyalists who grew rich in steam navigation. It is among the finest and the largest of

Kingston's surviving stone homes. Balls were held on its second floor when one of the Gildersleeves was mayor in 1855–56. It now houses business offices.

At William Street, our walk passes into the Old Sydenham Ward, which contains Kingston's greatest concentration of stone buildings. On either side of the south intersection there are vintage structures, originally put up as banks. The Empire Life office was the Commercial Bank (1853) and the Frontenac Club Apartments was the Bank of Montreal (1845). Attorney John S. Cartwright built his law office in 1834 farther along the same block, and Knaresborough Cottage, at 203 King Street East, dates from the same year.

Another of Kingston's limestone jewels is the Cartwright House, at the southwest corner of King and Gore Streets. It was built by Rev. Robert D. Cartwright in 1833 and has come down the years remarkably unchanged. In front of Earl Place, at 156 King Street East, look for the city's last gas street lamp. The home was built by Hugh Earl, who married Chief Joseph Brant's niece. Between here and West Street several interesting structures stand but as you approach the intersection the prevailing style begins to shade into Victorian. This is the City Park area. Several fine mansions surround the park, which opens out on Lake Ontario at its southern boundary. At the foot of West Street is the Pump House, built in 1849 as part of the city's waterworks and now housing a museum of steam engines. The huge engines that once ran the machinery in the building are restored to their 1897 glory. Open mid-June to mid-September; admission charge. Another interesting old house with a fine view over the lake is Edgewater House at the foot of Emily Street, west of the park. It dates from the 1850s.

That squat structure in the park near the foot of Barrie Street is the Murney Tower, an armed redoubt constructed in 1846. It was part of the general defense system of the Kingston area, expanded then during a period of friction with the United States. Known officially as a martello tower, it is named after a form of fortification that originated in Corsica. The walls are fifteen feet thick at the base and twelve feet at the top, another handy use for the local limestone. Open daily in July and August; weekends in June and September. There is an admission charge.

Walk north along Barrie Street. At the head of the park is the dome of the county courthouse, another building from the 1850s. Turn left on Stuart Street and then just beyond Arch Street turn right into the walkway to Queen's University. Founded in 1841, the university presents a harmonious grouping of its limestone buildings on this central quad. Notice in particular the medieval cluster of the Theological Building, the Grant Hall campanile and the Victorian-Romanesque pile of Ontario Hall. Across University Avenue and south toward Queen's Crescent is the Agnes Etherington Art Centre with permanent displays. Open 9:00 to 5:00, weekdays; 1:00 to 5:00, weekends; free.

Follow Queen's Crescent to Lower Albert Street, then turn left to get back to King Street. In a few more blocks you will reach Centre Street and a right turn will take you to the most famous house in the city, Bellevue. It bears no resemblance at all to the limestone dwellings elsewhere in Kingston. It is instead almost a madcap Italianate villa, although built about the same time as the others. The house is a National Historic Park, though, because for two years it was the residence of John A. Macdonald, first prime minister of Canada. Grocer Charles Hales built Bellevue in 1838–40 and it was known by the local wits as the "Pekoe Pagoda." Macdonald, then a young member of the legislative assembly, moved in as a tenant with his ailing wife and infant son in 1848. The baby died, Mrs. Macdonald continued to fail, and Macdonald moved out in 1849 during a temporary reverse in his rising political career. But brief and unhappy as his residency was, the attractiveness of the house itself can justify its exalted status today. It was impossible to reassemble articles belonging to Macdonald, so the home is furnished in a style that would have been favored by a mildly prosperous family of the time. It is made to look lived-in, too, with clothing strewn on the beds and such. A small exhibit room on the upper floor gives a biographical sketch of Macdonald. The house is open daily, 10:00 to 5:00; free.

Old Fort Henry

There is a disconcerting element of tripping through time in visiting Fort Henry. You approach the entrance to the advanced battery enclosure and a sentry springs to attention and snaps off a rather startling salute, "Welcome to Fort Henry, sir. Is this your first visit?" At the main gateway to the fort itself another tourist with a camera approaches an area that could be danger-ous and a sentry begins to bawl for his commander. That officer shows up and asks the tourist to back off a bit, thank you.

Within the fort other soldiers, some in nineteenth-century British uniform, others in contemporary fatigues of tee-shirt and jeans, run this way and that on mysterious missions to various parts of the vast enclosure. A towering, dramatically sideburned young man in officer's regalia leads a group over to some bleachers set up along one side of the parade square. Suddenly, an alarm sounds and uniformed soldiers begin running from every corner. They line up, march to the ramparts on the double, prepare one of the batteries for firing, and let fly a mock charge. At least, they tell you it is a mock charge. There is a moment or two when you are not so sure. Just as everything else about Fort Henry, it looks as realistic as the present century can manage.

Fort Henry is a living museum. The soldiers are actually local college students who work as guides during the summer months as members of the Fort Henry Guard. They take it quite seriously. They must pass examinations in drill to qualify and they memorize a small textbook full of information about the old fort to act as tour guides. Their retreat pageants, held at 7:30 P.M. each Wednesday and Saturday during July and August, may well be the best display of military pageantry extant in North America. There is a fife-and-drum concert, an exhibition of 1867 military drill, a mock battle complete with artillery discharges, and finally a ceremonial lowering of the flag. If you do not respond to all that with chills down your spine, better stick to John Wayne movies.

Fort Henry occupies a bluff above the city of Kingston,

commanding the entrance to the St. Lawrence River from Lake Ontario. It is certainly one of the most strategic locations on the continent. Construction of the fort began almost immediately after the American declaration of war in the summer of 1812. Its original purpose was to protect the naval dockyard at Kingston, one of the primary objectives of the American forces in the indecisive Lake Ontario campaign. The original fort was something of a slapdash affair. But when the Rideau Canal was built in 1829, connecting Kingston and Ottawa by an interior waterway, the colonial government recognized the necessity for an improved defense system. Construction of an enlarged fort was approved and completed in 1836. It is essentially the same fort that stands today.

For the next thirty-four years Fort Henry was manned by thirty-three different imperial regiments before being turned over to Canada. Although relations with the United States had their edgy moments, the fort never fired a shot in battle, and hardly ever in anger. It was strengthened during the early 1840s, when the advanced battery was added, and again at the time of the Oregon Crisis in 1845, when a series of martello towers were built at various points around Kingston for defense (see pages 77–78). The fort's martellos were completed a few months after the signing of the Oregon Treaty.

Its major use seems to have been as a prison. Followers of William Lyon Mackenzie were interned here after the rebellion of 1837 and one of them was hung there. Although it was abandoned as a military post in 1890, its old quarters were used to house German prisoners in both world wars.

Today, the officers' quarters have been restored to their appearance of the 1860s, the same period from which the uniforms of the Fort Henry Guard were drawn. The fort operates on a daily routine much as it would have in those years— even to the extent of bakers and tailors servicing the Guard in the manner of the previous century.

It is living history at its best, a thrilling and educational step back into the past. The views of Kingston from its outer works are magnificent, too. Fort Henry is open daily from mid-May to mid-October, but there are no Guard ceremonies after mid-

September. Hours are 9:30 to 5:00 through mid-June; 9:30 to 6:30, through Labor Day (except for the Wednesday and Saturday night retreat ceremonies, weather permitting); and 9:30 to 5:00 thereafter. There is an admission charge.

Members of the Fort Henry Guard maintain the old military post in the manner of the nineteenth century. *Courtesy the* Detroit Free Press.

Quinte's Isle

A few miles east of the town of Picton there is a hill and on the top of the hill there is a lake. The lake is something of a mystery. It apparently has no source. It is just there, the Lake on the Mountain, sparkling away in the sunshine amid the cries of happy picnickers who are not overly concerned about its source.

The lake, in a way, is a reflection of the character of all of Quinte's Isle, that slab of land that drops into Lake Ontario from the regular shoreline of the north coast. In a highly developed, commercially active section of Ontario, there suddenly appears an area that belongs to another time. It seems to have no connection at all with the bustling mainland that lies just across the three short bridges and causeways. There are fruit farms here, and some good cheese is produced at Waupoos, and the waters teem with bass and pike, pickerel and muskie. There are four provincial parks on Quinte's Isle and tourism thrives. But it is a very sedate kind of tourism, directed at families and those who wish to turn away for a time from the tumult that lies just beyond the bridges.

Lake on the Mountain is probably the busiest part of the isle. Besides the lake there is a fine view over the Bay of Quinte, enlivened by the little government ferry that runs every few minutes between Glenora on the island and Adolphustown on the mainland. Picton, the county town, has its bustling corners on summer weekends. It also has a county courthouse that was built in Greek-revival style in 1833 and is still being used for the same purpose today.

That is more in keeping with the atmosphere on the isle. From Picton it is quite easy to strike out in any direction and in a matter of minutes be absolutely nowhere. This is a wonderful quality for any area to possess and one to be treasured. Head southeast on the county road and you will eventually come to Waupoos (it means rabbit in Indian). An island of the same name lies just offshore and there are drives along Smith Bay and to the Black River cheddar cheese factory. Drive south from Picton on another county road and you will arrive at South Bay where there is a mariner's museum and a road out to the lighthouse on Long Point.

Drive north from Picton on Highway 49 and there will be scenic overlooks of the Bay of Quinte. A mile from town the White Chapel, built in 1809, marks the site of the oldest Methodist church in Ontario. An intriguing graveyard lies behind the peaceful old church.

A drive west will take you to the island's beaches at Sandbanks, Outlet Beach, and North Beach Provincial Parks. Sandbanks, with its 1,200 acres of dunes and long stretches of sandy beach, is especially scenic.

This is the heart of Loyalist country. Many of the farms are still worked by the descendants of the original families who landed here in 1784 after leaving New York State across the lake. Wellington, on a bluff above the lake, is the prettiest of the villages that they founded. Several of them have museums containing the crafts and artifacts of the pioneers in the area. There is one at Maryburgh, near Waupoos; another at Wellington; and still another on the northern part of the island, in Ameliasburgh, housed in a limestone church built in 1868.

Many sheltered bays in the area make it one of the top locales for sailing in Canada. Quinte also has more than its fair share of antique stores for bargain hunters. But you do not have to pursue any of these activities. All you really should do is follow one of those narrow country roads that lead to nowhere in particular, pull off at a likely looking place near the water, and think about that lake up on the mountain and what its source might possibly be. Think about it for a good, long time, too.

Other Things to See

[1]   Port Hope has managed to maintain one of the best-preserved nineteenth-century commercial districts in Canada. The architecture of its business section has been the subject of a Canadian Broadcasting Company documentary. Queen Elizabeth was also a visitor to this charming town and attended Sunday services in St. Mark's Church in 1959. The tiny church dates from 1822.

[2]   Cobourg was once a great rival to Toronto. When the latter city built its St. Lawrence Hall, Cobourg responded with Victoria Hall. Regarded as one of Ontario's finest neoclassic buildings, the recently restored hall housed the city offices and courts. The restoration includes a cafe, historic courtroom, assembly hall, and a hall of fame of Cobourg residents.

[3]   Probably the most famed of these was Marie Dressler, the actress who costarred with Wallace Beery in the "Min and Bill" films of the 1930s. Her birthplace, on the west side of Cobourg, is now the Old Canadian Eating House and Tavern, a Victorian style restaurant. Other actresses with local associations were Katharine Cornell, who spent girlhood summer vacations here with relatives, and Beatrice Lillie, who lived here for a time and appeared in performances at Victoria Hall.

[4]   Victoria Park is a pleasant twenty-five-acre facility on the Cobourg lakefront. It is enlivened during the summer months with Tuesday evening concerts by the Cobourg Kiltie Band. The town also hosts Highland games on the first Saturday of each July in Donegan Park.

[5]   Mill owner Eliakim Barnum built his Georgian home just west of Grafton in 1817 after British troops accidentally burned down the original during the War of 1812. It now is a museum of the area, besides being an architectural monument in its own right. Open 1:00 to 5:00, daily, July and August; 1:00 to 5:00 Sundays and holidays in May, June, September, and October. There is an admission charge.

[6]   One of the great inland waterways on the continent, the Trent-Severn Canal has its Lake Ontario outlet in Trenton. About 240 miles and forty-five locks to the northwest it empties

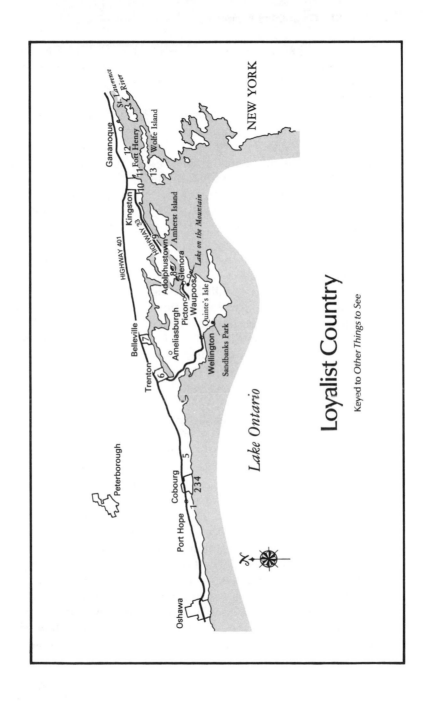

Loyalist Country

Keyed to Other Things to See

Peterborough

Oshawa

Port Hope

Cobourg

1

234

5

HIGHWAY 401

Trenton

6

Belleville

7

Ameliasburgh

Picton

Adolphustown

Glenora

Waupoos

Wellington

Sandbanks Park

Quinte's Isle

Lake on the Mountain

Amherst Island

HIGHWAY 33

HIGHWAY 2

8

9

Kingston

10

11

12

Fort Henry

13

Gananoque

St. Lawrence River

Wolfe Island

NEW YORK

Lake Ontario

into Georgian Bay at Port Severn, passing through Lake Simcoe en route. Following the winding course of the waterway is regarded as one of the top boating adventures in the Great Lakes area.

[7]   Belleville is a favorite harbor for sailors on the Bay of Quinte, which is an outstanding cruising area. It also houses a good regional museum in Glanmore House, a handsomely restored Victorian mansion. Open Tuesday through Saturday, 9:00 to 4:00; Sunday, 1:00 to 5:00 in July and August. Tuesday through Sunday, 1:00 to 5:00, the rest of the year; admission charge. Two miles north of town in Corbyville, the Corby Distillery provides daily tours at 10:00 and 2:00, May to mid-July; weekends only, August and September; free.

[8]   The Loyalist Memorial Church preserves the banners of Loyalist military units in its wood-beamed interior and the names of the founding families are inscribed on its walls. A memorial tower is adjacent to the church in Adolphustown, a few miles east of the ferry dock to Quinte's Isle on Highway 33. A lakefront park also contains a Loyalist museum and preserves the graves of several original settlers who landed here in 1784.

[9]   Highway 33 between Quinte's Isle ferry and Kingston is an outstanding scenic drive, with beautiful views of the lake and of Amherst Island.

[10]   When Canada established a federal penitentiary on Lake Ontario in 1833, the village of Portsmouth grew up around it. It turned into a showcase for local architect William Coverdale, whose limestone buildings dot the former village which was absorbed by Kingston in 1952. Notable are the Village Hall, located on the green across King Street from the prison; St. John's Church on Church Street near Yonge Street; and a row of houses on the harborfront recently restored by the city. Portsmouth has the look and feel of an English seaside town and is ideal for a leisurely walk. Its harbor was the site of the boating events in the 1976 Olympics.

[11]   The Royal Military College was founded in 1876 on the point of land between Fort Henry and Kingston. Fort Frederick originally occupied the site and one of its martello towers now houses a museum of the college and of Canada's military

history. Open daily, 9:00 to 9:00; June 1 to Labor Day; admission charge. The rest of the college grounds is open to visitors but none of the buildings is.

[12]   Just east of the Highway 2 turnoff to Fort Henry is the Vimy Barracks, containing the unique Royal Canadian Signals Museum. The exhibits trace the history of military communications all the way back to ancient Greece. Open daily, May through September; open Tuesday through Friday and Sunday, the rest of the year. Closed the last two weeks of December. Donation asked.

[13]   Ferryboats leave from downtown Kingston to Wolfe Island, the first and largest of the Thousand Islands of the St. Lawrence River. You can then drive across the island and catch a boat for Cape Vincent, New York, on the far side. The Hitchcock House, built in 1832, operates as an inn on Wolfe Island.

Side Trips

Serpent Mounds Provincial Park preserves an elongated Indian mound which might have been used for burials. It is on the shore of Rice Lake, just south of Keene, about 40 miles north of Cobourg via Highway 45 and county roads. In the same vicinity, north of Keene, is Century Village, a collection of fourteen Ontario pioneer structures. Open mid-May to mid-October.

Peterborough is the administrative center of the Trent-Severn Waterway and there are cruises through its sixty-five-foot high hydraulic lift lock. The two-hour cruise also passes by Trent University. Daily from July to mid-September. The city is 35 miles north-northwest of Cobourg on Highway 28.

At Healey Falls, the Trent-Severn Waterway passes through three locks right alongside a pleasant waterfall. About 37 miles from Trenton via Highways 401, 30, and a county road out of Campbellford.

The Thousand Islands begin at Kingston's back door but they belong more properly to the St. Lawrence Valley than the Great Lakes area. Cruises from the Kingston area into the famed scenic area operate during the summer months. The *Miss Kings-*

ton and *Lady Kingston,* operated by Miss Kingston Boat Lines, take four-and-one-half-hour cruises through the islands daily from late May to late September. The dock is four miles east of Kingston on Highway 2. Check locally for times and rates in effect.

Other cruises leave from Gananoque—21 miles east of Kingston—and Rockport—about 35 miles east. Gananoque Boat Lines has a three-hour trip aboard a paddle-wheeler from early May to mid-October. Also leaving from Gananoque's Customs Dock is International Boat Lines, operating over the same time period. Rockport Boat Lines, just east of the International Bridge, operates cruises from mid-May to mid-October. Check locally for times and fares in each case.

To see the islands from land, take the Thousand Islands Parkway, a scenic drive that cuts off from Highway 401 east of Gananoque. On the International Bridge to the United States, the Skydeck presents vistas over the islands from a height of 350 feet. It is about 37 miles from Kingston. Open 9:00 to 6:00, mid-May to mid-October; until sunset in the summer months. There is an admission charge.

Kingston is the outlet for the Rideau Canal, built as an interior communications system in the event of war in 1829. Now it is an excursion for pleasure boaters between Lake Ontario and the nation's capital on the Ottawa River.

Provincial Parks on Lake Ontario

Darlington—26 miles west of Port Hope, has picnicking, boating, swimming, and 400 campsites.

Presqu'ile—12 miles west of Trenton, has complete recreational facilities, with a mile-long sand beach, wildlife sanctuary, aquarium, natural history museum, and a visitor's center in the onetime home of the lighthouse caretaker. There are 500 campsites.

North Beach—on the northwest corner of Quinte's Isle, 14 miles south of Trenton, has picnic grounds, swimming, and fishing. No camping.

Sandbanks—9 miles southwest of Picton, has a complete recreational setup and 50 campsites. (See page 83.)

Outlet Beach—10 miles southwest of Picton, has a 2-mile sand beach, picnicking, boating, and 480 campsites.

Lake on the Mountain—5 miles east of Picton, has picnicking. No camping. (See page 82.)

Adolphustown—30 miles west of Kingston, has recreational facilities, a Loyalist museum and memorial, and 82 campsites.

If you go for a weekend: Stay in Kingston.
1. Tour Old Fort Henry.
2. Take the walk outlined in this chapter.
3. Go on one of the cruises through the Thousand Islands.

If you go for a week: Stay in Kingston for three nights, in Picton for two, and in Cobourg for two.

1–3. Same as the weekend tour.

4. Visit the Royal Military College and Museum. Drive west to Portsmouth and explore the area. Continue west on Highway 33, past the Loyalist Memorial Church, and catch the ferry to Quinte's Isle.

5. Enjoy the beaches and villages of Quinte's Isle.

6. Drive to Belleville to see the Glanmore House and visit the Corby Distillery. Proceed west on Highway 2 to Cobourg to see Victoria Hall.

7. Take a side trip to Serpent Mounds Provincial Park and to Peterborough for a cruise through the hydraulic lift lock.

George Eastman's stately mansion on Rochester's East Avenue now houses a museum of photography. *Courtesy New York State Travel Bureau.*

Land of the Iroquois

During the long decades of exploration and settlement of the North American continent, the colonial powers stayed far away from the Lake Ontario shoreline of New York. The intrepid French established their trading routes to the North along the Ottawa River and then by portage to Lake Huron, rather than traveling along Lake Ontario. British settlement from the East reached as far as the Mohawk Valley and then stopped.

The reason? This part of New York was the home of the Iroquois, the dreaded Five Nations Confederacy, the most feared Indian power in colonial America. These five peoples—the Senecas, Cayugas, Oneidas, Onondagas, and Mohawks—were aggressive and skilled at war. And they would as soon war on encroaching Europeans as on neighboring tribes. They exterminated the Eriez Indians in one campaign, leaving only that tribe's name behind on one of the Great Lakes. Another of the Lakes tribes, the Huron, was drawn to an alliance with the French because of their fear and hatred of the Iroquois.

The Iroquois hostility toward the French went back to their initial encounter with Samuel de Champlain in 1609. Moving out of New France with a force of Hurons and Algonquins, he

91

collided with the Iroquois. Two chiefs were killed by musket fire before Champlain retreated, and the Iroquois became implacable enemies of the French for as long as they remained in North America. Their trading parties played havoc with the fur trade and took a terrible toll on France's Indian allies. Finally, in 1687, the Marquis de Denonville, governor of New France, decided things had gone far enough. Assembling the largest French force seen on the continent to that time, he landed at Irondequoit Bay at the mouth of the Genesee River. He established a fort there, marched overland to the Niagara to start another outpost, fought Indians, and burned villages on the · way. But when he left, the Iroquois returned to take control of the land, hating the French with an even deeper passion.

Their enmity gave the Iroquois a natural cause for aligning with the British. After the French and Indian War resulted in the defeat of their longtime enemies, the Iroquois saw even greater reason for maintaining this alliance. They were aware of the expanding settlements on their eastern borders and knew the colonials coveted their lands. So at the start of the Revolution, the Iroquois under their chief Joseph Brant remained loyal to Britain. But not all of the confederacy did. The Oneidas and the Tuscaroras (a later addition to the confederacy) joined the rebels or remained neutral. When an Iroquois force was routed with the British at Oriskany, a deep wedge was driven into the Indian confederacy. Their raiding parties did so much damage, though, that the colonists were obliged to send a force under General John Sullivan into the Iroquois lands.

In a devastating campaign through the summer of 1779, Sullivan carried on a war of attrition through the Genesee Valley, burning the Iroquois crops and villages. The expedition fell short of its goal, the capture of the Loyalist base at Fort Niagara. But it accomplished something even more dangerous to the Iroquois. It gave the land-hungry New Englanders in Sullivan's command a look at the rich lands of the Genesee. After the war, nothing could keep them out.

Many of the Iroquois followed Brant into Canada, but the Seneca remained. Conflicting claims on the land were settled by New York and Massachusetts and soon afterward the buyers came. Highway 14, running from Sodus Bay to the Pennsylvania line, marks the eastern border of this rich area. It would include the future city of Rochester and Lake Ontario frontage all the way to Troutburg. After a rapid succession of land deals engineered by financier Robert Morris, the bulk of the land wound up in the hands of British and Dutch development companies. A 1797 treaty with the Senecas obliterated the last Indian claims, the tracts were opened for purchase and the settlers poured in. Today, the once mighty Iroquois survive here only as names on the land—lakes, and counties, and towns— the same fate they had inflicted on their Indian neighbors centuries before.

The construction of the Erie Canal touched off an enormous land boom in the area. Rochester, lying squarely athwart the canal route, was transformed from a mill town at the falls of the Genesee into a rich, young giant. As it happened, Rochester became the only city of consequence on the New York shore of Lake Ontario. And even Rochester's lake frontage is only an appendage to the city, not an important part of its economic history. The lakefront is more fully used as recreation land. The majority of the New York shore is taken up by fruit farms, with large areas in celery production as well.

Ridge Road, Highway 104, marking the end of Lake Ontario's glacial plain, is the historic highway west through this part of the country. North of Oswego, the lakefront is almost entirely recreation land, culminating in the major resort area of the Thousand Islands.

The Eastman Empire and Rochester

There was a Rochester before there was a George Eastman; just as there was a Detroit before Henry Ford or a Philadelphia before Benjamin Franklin. But it was a far different city from the one it became after he lived there. Like Ford and Franklin, Eastman stamped his city with his genius so that afterward it would be difficult to think of the place without associating it immediately with the man.

Eastman's invention and marketing of roll film and the Kodak camera here is the single most significant event in the history of Rochester's development. Not that the city was otherwise populated exclusively by nonentities. Far from it. Susan B. Anthony, the tireless crusader for women's rights lived here. So did Frederick Douglass, the escaped slave who edited his abolitionist newspaper here. So did Bausch and Lomb, who began their optical glass company here. So did Hiram Sibley who started Western Union. But it is still the look of Eastman that the city wears today.

Rochester began as a mill on the Genesee River operated by an unsavory character named Ebenezer Allan, known as "Indian" to his friends, of whom there were very few. A Loyalist during the Revolution, Allan was a self-confessed murderer and polygamist when he arrived in the Genesee Valley in 1782. About six years later he was given a 100-acre tract to operate a sawmill and gristmill at the falls of the Genesee in what is now the heart of downtown Rochester. But no one was about to name a city after Ebenezer Allan. His holdings were absorbed by Robert Morris in 1791 and Allan moved to Upper Canada and disappeared. It was not until 1811 that Nathaniel Rochester came from Maryland, began laying out lots in the area, and had the city named after him.

The mills that Allan started proliferated to such an extent after construction of the Erie Canal, that Rochester was popularly known as the "Flour City." Later in the century, as the milling industry followed the grainfields west, Rochester turned to indoor nurseries for income and the spelling was changed to the "Flower City." Then in 1888 came Eastman and his Brownie.

The development of the Kodak and celluloid film made photography a popular pastime and turned Eastman, the son of a penmanship teacher, into an extremely wealthy man. By the time of his death by his own hand in 1932, he had given away $72 million of his earnings. Much of it went to his hometown and to the University of Rochester which he virtually turned with his checkbook into a major educational facility. Music and medicine were his personal preferences.

There are three places in particular in Rochester where one can gauge the effect Eastman had on his community. The first would be the Eastman Theater, at East Main and Gibbs streets, downtown. Built with an Eastman grant in 1922, the theater is still one of the most acoustically perfect halls in the country. It is the center of the city's musical life and a showcase for the Eastman School of Music at the University of Rochester which, again through Eastman's largesse, is among the finest in the world. From October to early August, free concerts and recitals are held in the theater by students and faculty from the School of Music. You are likely to see, at any given time, performances of jazz, choral, and instrumental music or opera. Check with the concert manager's office at 26 Gibbs Street for times and dates. The school also performs opera under the stars every July and August in the Highland Park Bowl, in the southern part of the city.

East Avenue was the preferred address of Rochester's wealthiest families and at the turn of the century it was lined with grand homes. Eastman built one of the grandest in 1905, a fifty-room Georgian showplace at 900 East Avenue. Since his death the mansion has been turned into a museum of photography. Many of Eastman's possessions and paintings remain, giving the George Eastman House a homelike atmosphere, too. There are extensive exhibits concerning the mechanical and physical aspects of both still and motion picture photography. But the high point is the collection of historic photographs on the upper floors. They freeze for an instant one fragment of a past that is gone forever and in so doing preserve the instant for the ages. Historian Daniel Boorstin observed that Eastman's invention changed the way we look at the past. "Instead of merely photographing persons or scenes that were especially memorable or historic," he wrote, "Americans would photograph at random and then remember the scenes because they had been photographed. Photography became a device for making experience worth remembering." And these long ago experiences are shared once again with us in the George Eastman House. The house is open between 10:00 and 5:00 Tuesday to Sunday. There is an admission charge.

The third stop of the Eastman tour should be Kodak Park, at 200 Ridge Road West, in the city's northern section. Eastman purchased sixteen acres in what was then countryside in 1891 in order to install his manufacturing plants. The site now encompasses 2,000 acres. More than 28,000 people are employed in 170 buildings in this self-contained city and another 20,000 work for Eastman Kodak in other plants around Rochester. Kodak Park tours are given on weekdays at 9:30 and 1:30, except for holidays, and two or three installations are visited over a course of some ninety minutes. Free, and well worthwhile if only to see the sensitive conditions under which people who deal with film must work.

Kodak, by the way, is a name thought up by Eastman himself. He was seeking a trademark that would be unique, unmistakable and easy to pronounce. He also liked the sound of the letter *k*, which seemed full of action and decisiveness to him. So after trying out various combinations of letters between an opening and a concluding *k*, the word Kodak is what he came up with. One further note. There are no cameras allowed on the Kodak plant tours.

Oswego and Fort Ontario

Had things turned out a bit differently, Oswego, not Buffalo, would be the second largest city in New York today. Instead of a pleasant lakeside town of some 20,000 people, Oswego would be about twenty times as big and one of the busiest ports on the Great Lakes. But a report that was compiled in 1809 determined that the future of Oswego would be a peaceful one—at least as far as commerce was concerned. When it came to warfare, however, the history of Oswego and its Fort Ontario has been anything but peaceful.

Because of its strategic location, at the southeastern extremity of Lake Ontario with water connections into the heart of New York, it has always been a focal point of conflict. Those were the very same factors that made it the logical lake terminus for the Erie Canal when plans for the waterway were being discussed in the early years of the nineteenth century. On the map, Oswego would appear to be the only conceivable choice. Water traffic from the East reaches it easily along the Mohawk River, Oneida Lake, and the Oswego River. The route would have been about 200 miles shorter and present far fewer obstacles and variances in elevation than a Lake Erie outlet. But two factors lined up against it, more political than geographical. One was the powerful Holland Land Company with its vast holdings west of Sodus Bay. For the company to make any profit from the canal it had to pass through its holdings and empty into Lake Erie. An outlet at Oswego to Lake Ontario did the company no good at all. The company lobbied vigorously for the Lake Erie route.

Another consideration was of equal significance. How much cargo would be diverted to Canadian ports if ships from the west were not pulled immediately into New York at Lake Erie? American officials feared the loss would be considerable. So when surveyor James Geddes turned in his route recommendations in 1809, he favored the Lake Erie outlet. The Holland Land Company promptly kicked in with a 100,000-acre gift to the state and surveying assistance, and everyone was happy. Except for Oswego, that is. The canal to the south pulled virtually all water commerce, including its bustling market in salt shipments, away from Oswego. A cut-off eventually was built to Oswego and the city recovered a portion of the traffic. But nothing like it might have been had Oswego, and not Buffalo, been the canal outlet.

Oswego today is a rather attractive place with a business district built along both sides of its river, a few impressive public buildings, and a particularly nice green surrounded by houses of worship. There is a fine park situated on bluffs above the lake to the west of the river. The city also has a fine historical museum in the ornate Richardson-Bates House, at 135 East Third Street, in an area of rambling old homes. It is open between 1:00 and 5:00, Tuesday to Sunday, July to Labor Day; Wednesday and weekends only, mid-May to June and Labor Day to mid-October. Call in advance for times the rest of the year. There is no admission charge.

The history of Oswego is mostly wrapped up in the fort at the foot of East Seventh Street, restored now to its appearance of the Civil War era. The site was first fortified in 1755 and was a center of conflict in three wars. Unlike other Great Lakes installations that rarely if ever were actually involved in battle, Fort Ontario was in the thick of things at every outbreak of hostilities.

The first fort in the area was situated on the western side of the river, near that pleasant lakeside park. The British built Fort Oswego in the wilderness in 1727 as a check on French ambitions in the area. It was joined twenty-eight years later by Forts George and Ontario as war between the two colonial powers became imminent. One year later, in 1756, the French moved against the three forts under the leadership of their commander in chief, Louis Joseph de Montcalm. He took and leveled all three outposts within four days. Before they fell, though, the British did succeed in putting their first naval vessel on the Great Lakes at the site.

Three years later, the British returned to the abandoned site and rebuilt Fort Ontario under Sir William Johnson and Jeffrey Amherst. The fort was used as a base for Johnson's successful siege of Fort Niagara and for Amherst's expedition that ended in the fall of Montreal.

As the Revolution approached, the fort again figured promi-
nently in British plans. Iroquois leader Joseph Brant concluded
his alliance with Britain here and General St. Leger left the fort
in 1777 to begin his planned campaign against New England.
He was stopped and routed at Oriskany, though, and the badly
shaken British again abandoned Fort Ontario. But five years
later they were back once more, unwilling to relinquish a
position with such strategic possibilities. It withstood a colonial
assault and remained in British hands until 1796 when it was
surrendered with all the other frontier outposts they had refused
to give up after the Revolution. The settlement of the town of
Oswego begins from that time.

But war was not yet finished with Fort Ontario. In May,
1814, the British landed again and managed to seize the fort.
The American forces withdrew to the falls of the Oswego River
but the British had been so badly mauled during their landing
that they were unable to hold the fort. They destroyed it instead
and sailed off.

This time the fort remained a ruin for twenty-five years until
renewed conflicts on the border occasioned its final reconstruction. This installation is the fort that stands today. Its barracks,
ramparts, and bastions may be inspected, and a museum occupies the upper floor of the enlisted men's barracks. The fort
remained an active military post until 1946 when it was acquired by the state of New York. It survives as a token of one of
the most bitterly contested pieces of property in the country's
early history. Open mid-May to October, Monday through Saturday from 9:00 to 5:00; Sunday from 1:00 to 5:00. There is an
admission charge.

Sackets Harbor

Although it scarcely looks the part today, tiny Sackets Harbor was once a vital American military base, one of the most important on the Great Lakes. The first shots of the War of 1812 were fired here and in the nearby Madison Barracks such illustrious generals as Ulysses S. Grant and John Pershing once served as junior officers.

Sackets Harbor now is a pleasant resort town on the indented coastline of eastern Lake Ontario. Large, irregularly shaped peninsulas jut far out into the water, sheltering bays for ideal sailing, while the lake surface is broken by clusters of islands, forerunners of the Thousand Islands that lie just a few miles to the north.

The state of New York is undertaking an ambitious historical program here, an addition to the battlefield park that has been open since 1933. The Union Hotel, a fine federal-era stone building that is considered the best surviving structure of its kind in upper New York, was restored in 1976. Next on the agenda is the refurbishing of the Augustus Sacket house, built by the founder of the town in 1802. Other early nineteenth-century buildings run along Main Street and, presumably, in the next few years will take on tourist-related functions to complement the adjacent reconstructions.

Already in operation is the Pickering-Beach Historical Museum, next to the battlefield at the head of Main Street. Built in 1817 by a prominent state family as a summer home, it contains exhibits relating to local history and some memorabilia of U.S. Grant. It remained in the hands of the original family, whose progeny included a lieutenant-governor of New York, until 1936. Open Memorial Day to Labor Day between 10:00 and 5:00. There is an admission charge.

It is the battlefield, however, that is the featured point of interest here. One month after the formal declaration of war, in July, 1812, a British fleet suddenly appeared off the town, which was busily transforming itself into the primary American shipyard on Lake Ontario. The small defending force wheeled out the biggest gun it could find, an unwieldy piece of ordnance nicknamed the "Old Sow." Ungainly as it was, the gun inflicted sufficient damage on the invaders to convince them to withdraw. That gave the Americans the breathing space they needed to begin operations at the shipyard.

The following May the British returned and this time they managed to land troops. Before they could destroy the shipyard, a small unit of militia arrived. The British feared this was the vanguard of a major American force and they returned to their ships before they could inflict significant damage. Again Sackets Harbor was saved. A series of maps and markers on the waterfront explains the maneuvers during the two battles and a museum in the commandant's house presents additional information about Sackets Harbor's importance in those years. Open June to Labor Day between 9:00 and 9:00. There is no admission charge.

Even though the battles fought here were far from decisive, Sackets Harbor played a central role in the strange Lake Ontario campaign. Although there was no lack of terrible and bloody battles on land, both naval commanders on the lake seemed determined to avoid a confrontation on water at all costs. Sir James Yeo and Captain Isaac Chauncey instead were content to have their respective shipyards fight the war. The campaign here turned into a ship construction contest. Every time one side gained a superiority in tonnage, leading to expectations of imminent battle, the other side would turn out a new ship, too, and the two commanders would back away again. It went on like that for years. Actually, it may be the best way imaginable of fighting a war. It kept casualties to a minimum, and aside from exhausting the overburdened shipyard workers, no one was much the worse for wear. On the rare occasions when the enemy fleets came within hailing distance, there would generally be a few shots fired and then one side would break away to open water. Usually this was followed up by statements from the opposing commander, accusing the enemy of showing a lack of spirit. A very odd campaign, to say the least.

One of the strangest mementos of the war was the hull of the battleship *New Orleans,* which was intended as the crowning achievement of the Sackets Harbor shipyards. If Chauncey ever had managed to put it afloat there probably would have been plenty of action on the lake. But the war was finished before the *New Orleans* was and for years afterward, the ship, which was planned as the largest built on the Lakes up to that time, remained at its berth as a tourist curiosity. It even served as a hotel for a time before its destruction late in the century.

The Madison Barracks, just west of town off New York 3, were built during one of the periodic eruptions of border tensions with Canada in the 1840s. The base was abandoned in 1946 but the red brick military structures still stand, like a vast ghost post. The gates are open and you can drive through the deserted base for one of the eeriest little trips in the Lakes area.

Other Things to See

[1]   Cobblestone was the major product of Childs, New York, and the Orleans County village plays tribute to it at the Cobblestone Society Museum. There is a church dating from 1834, a school from 1849, and a museum of cobblestone masonry at the junction of New York 104 (Ridge Road) and New York 98. Open July and August, Tuesday through Saturday, 11:00 to 5:00; Sunday, 1:00 to 5:00. Donation asked.

[2]   When the city of Rochester received its tax payment from the owner of the house at 17 Madison Street each year, there was always a note attached to it: "Paid under protest. Taxation without representation is tyranny." The homeowner was Susan B. Anthony who spent most of her life campaigning for women's suffrage using this house as her headquarters. She died in 1906, before the final victory was won in America. The home, just west of downtown, is a memorial to her and her associates in the long struggle. Open Wednesday through Saturday, 11:00 to 4:00; admission charge. Other times by appointment.

[3]   When the Erie Canal brought sudden prosperity to Rochester, many residents went out and built the best Greek revival home their new money could buy. The Campbell-Whittlesey House, dating from 1835, has been authentically restored and furnished in the manner of those boom years. It is located at 123 South Fitzhugh Street, in the southwestern corner of downtown. Open Tuesday through Friday, 10:00 to 5:00; Saturday and Sunday, 1:00 to 4:00. Closed in December. There is an admission charge.

[4]   Midtown Plaza is downtown Rochester's enclosed shopping mall, designed by architect Victor Gruen. Its centerpiece is the twenty-eight-foot high Clock of Nations which marks the hours with music and a puppet pageant. The mall is on East Main Street.

[5]   Right in back of the Plaza is Xerox Square, with changing exhibits on biology and the arts. It is near the corner of Broad and Clinton streets. Open Tuesday through Saturday, 10:00 to 7:00; Sunday, 1:00 to 5:00. Closed June to mid-September; free.

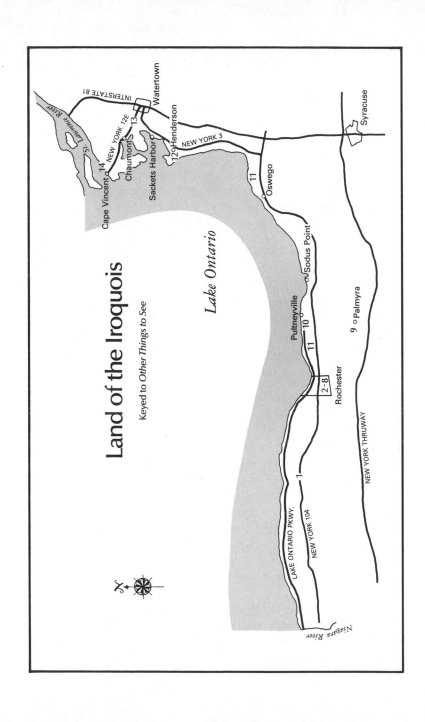

Land of the Iroquois

Keyed to *Other Things to See*

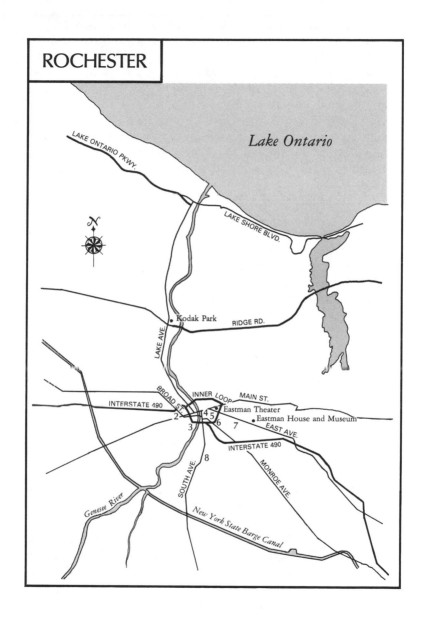

ROCHESTER

Lake Ontario

LAKE ONTARIO PKWY.

LAKE SHORE BLVD.

N

Kodak Park

LAKE AVE.

RIDGE RD.

BROAD ST.

INNER LOOP

MAIN ST.

INTERSTATE 490

Eastman Theater

2

4 5

3   6   7

Eastman House and Museum

EAST AVE.

INTERSTATE 490

8

SOUTH AVE.

MONROE AVE.

Genesee River

New York State Barge Canal

[6]   How America's cultural history was altered by the Industrial Revolution is the theme of an outstanding new museum in the southeastern corner of downtown Rochester. Located on Manhattan Square, the Margaret Woodbury Strong Museum houses her collection of 300,000 objects depicting the diversity of America's popular cultural experience from 1820 to 1930. The displays emphasize the Victorian period, but changing exhibits are planned as the wealth of material is inspected and organized. The museum is open Tuesday through Saturday, 10:00 to 5:00; Sunday, 1:00 to 5:00. There is an admission charge.

[7]   In the midst of the elegant homes of East Avenue, the Rochester Museum and Science Center contains outstanding exhibits of human biology, Indian cultures, Arctic life, and nineteenth-century Rochester. Open Monday through Saturday, from 9:00 to 5:00; Sunday, 1:00 to 5:00. Admission charge. Next door is the Strasenburgh Planetarium with its Star Theater. Shows at 8:00 P.M. on week nights; on the half hour from 1:30 to 3:30 on weekends with a 4:30 show on Sunday. Admission charge.

[8]   Lilac time in Rochester is something to behold. The city's lilac festival, usually held the third week of May, is centered around Highland Park, which contains 1,500 bushes of 535 varieties. It is on Highland Avenue, south of downtown. Botanic gardens and a conservatory in the park are open all year, daily, from 10:00 to 5:00.

[9]   When Joseph Smith found the Book of Mormon on Hill Cumorah, near Palmyra, American's largest home-grown religion was born. The hill is four miles south of town on New York 21, just north of New York Thruway, Exit 43. A statue of the Angel Moroni is now on the hill and the homes of Smith and a witness to the events on the hilltop, Martin Harris, are open daily, 8:00 to 6:00. A colorful pageant celebrating the founding of the Mormon religion is held on the hill each summer, in late July or early August. The Cumorah Mission in Rochester can provide dates and times for the events.

[10]   The county road along Lake Ontario in Wayne County is the most pleasant shoreline drive in the area. It wanders through lands purchased by Sir William Pulteney and the lakeside

The external architectural features of the Strasenburgh Planetarium are as interesting to view as the star shows and exhibits inside. Photograph from *Landmarks of Rochester and Monroe County*, by Paul Malo, copyright © 1974 by Syracuse University Press.

village named for him, Pultneyville, is a lovely stopping place for strolling and antiquing. The drive ends in the resort community of Sodus Point.

[11]   The Brookwood Science Information Center contains exhibits pertaining to nuclear energy and its applications. It is on Ontario Center Road, north from New York 104, east of Webster. Open Sunday through Thursday, 10:00 to 4:00 Easter to Thanksgiving; Sunday only, at other times; free. A similar facility, the Niagara-Mohawk Progress Center is located northeast of Oswego, north of New York 104. It contains a working model of a nuclear power plant. Open March through November, Tuesday through Saturday, from 10:00 to 5:00; Sunday, 12:00 to 6:00. Rest of year, Tuesday through Friday, 10:00 to 5:00.

[12]   There is a scenic lakeside drive to the resort town of Henderson Harbor, off New York 3, between Henderson and Sackets Harbor.

[13]   One of the most effective leaders in the War of 1812 was General Jacob Brown. His home in Brownville is open Wednesday, 2:00 to 5:00; Saturday, from 1:00 to 5:00; Tuesday and Friday, between 7:00 and 10:00 P.M.; free.

[14]   When Benjamin Franklin was in Paris, he was befriended by LeRays de Chaumont whose titled family was active in support of the American Revolution. After the French Revolution, Chaumont purchased land along Lake Ontario and in 1802 founded Cape Vincent, at the mouth of the St. Lawrence River. He intended it to be a great commercial rival to Kingston, across the river, and he brought in industrious French emigrés to settle here and in the nearby town of Chaumont. The colony failed after the Erie Canal diverted commerce to the south. Both towns are active resorts now with many of the stone homes of the original settlers, including Chaumont's own mansion in Cape Vincent, still standing. They are not open to the public, though. A lovely drive from Cape Vincent leads to Tibbett's Point and to the lighthouse that guards the entrance from Lake Ontario to the St. Lawrence River.

Side Trips
Letchworth State Park encompasses the gorge of the Genesee River, a scenic area of wooded hills and waterfalls. The

historic Glen Iris Inn puts up overnight guests within the park. The northern entrance at Mt. Morris is 37 miles south of Rochester via New York 15 and U.S. 20.

The Finger Lakes mark the map of central New York like the imprint of a giant hand. The region, which stretches south of a line between Rochester and Syracuse, includes some of the state's loveliest scenery and most interesting towns.

In Mumford, 20 miles southwest of Rochester, thirty-five structures from a twelve-county area of upstate New York have been assembled in a village setting to form Genesee County Museum. It is complete with everything from a church to a brewery. Open mid-May to mid-October, 10:00 to 5:00. There is an admission charge.

Canandaigua, 27 miles southeast of Rochester, has the Granger Homestead, home of the postmaster-general in the Jefferson and Madison administrations. It is open from 10:30 to 5:30, except on Monday. Also in town are the Sonnenberg Gardens, a series of ten formal gardens. Open mid-May through October, 10:00 to sundown.

In Geneva, 44 miles southeast of Rochester, is Rose Hill, a Greek-revival house dating from 1839 in a spectacular setting overlooking Seneca Lake. Open May through October, Monday through Saturday, 10:00 to 4:00; Sunday, 1:00 to 5:00. There is an admission charge.

In Waterloo, 46 miles southeast of Rochester, is the Memorial Day Museum, with items belonging to the cofounders of the national holiday which originated here. Open Memorial Day to Labor Day, Tuesday through Friday, 1:30 to 4:00. Two miles west of town stands the Scythe Tree, containing scythe blades embedded by local boys as they left for the Civil War and World War I.

In Auburn, 41 miles south of Oswego, is the Seward House, home of Lincoln's secretary of state. Open March through December, Monday through Saturday, 1:00 to 5:00. There is an admission charge.

In addition, there are scenic drives and state parks on most of the lakes.

The Thousand Islands area begins a few miles up the St. Lawrence River from Cape Vincent. Boat trips leave from Clayton,

15 miles east, and Alexandria Bay, 26 miles east. The American Boat Line operates from Clayton, late May to Labor Day. From Alexandria Bay, there are Uncle Sam Boat Tours, May through mid-October; and Paul Boat Line, May through September. Highlight of all the trips is a stop at Boldt Castle, a ruined, fairy tale castle on one of the islands. It was built by George C. Boldt for his wife who died while it was under construction. Heartbroken, he never had it completed.

State Parks on the Lake

Lakeside Beach—43 miles northwest of Rochester, on the Lake Ontario Parkway, has complete facilities for picnics and water sports, 12 cottages available for summer rental and 274 campsites.

Hamlin Beach—27 miles northwest of Rochester, has beaches, a cafe, concession stands, boating, and 266 campsites.

Braddock Bay—on the Lake Ontario Parkway, 13 miles northwest of Rochester, has complete day-use facilities.

Chimney Bluffs—on Sodus Bay, 36 miles southwest of Oswego, is a day-use park.

Two parks are located on either side of Oswego. On the west is Fairhaven Beach with 50 campsites, and on the east is Selkirk Shores, with 150 campsites.

Two state parks with beaches are just south of Sackets Harbor. Southwick Beach, about 20 miles south, has 66 campsites, and Westcott Beach, between Sackets Harbor and Henderson Harbor, has 122 campsites.

Long Point is on a peninsula that extends into the lake south of Cape Vincent. There are complete water facilities on Chaumont Bay and 63 campsites.

If you go for a weekend: Stay in Rochester.

1. Explore the downtown area and visit the Strong Museum.

2. Take the Kodak tour and see the Eastman House and Museum of photography.

3. Drive to the nearby Finger Lakes area for some of the attractions described in this chapter.

If you go for a week: Stay in Rochester four nights and in Watertown for three nights.

1–3. Same as the weekend tour.

4. Tour the Susan B. Anthony Home, the Campbell-Whittlesey House, and the Mormon historical sites in Palmyra.

5. Drive along the lakefront through Pultneyville and Sodus Point. Stop in Oswego to visit Fort Ontario and proceed to Watertown.

6. Tour Sackets Harbor. Relax on the beach at one of three state parks in the vicinity.

7. Drive to Alexandria Bay and take a Thousand Islands cruise.

The masts of Commodore Perry's flagship, *Niagara,* now tower above State Street in Erie, Pennsylvania. *Courtesy Tourist and Convention Bureau, Greater Erie Chamber of Commerce.*

5

From Buffalo to Erie

On a late October day in 1825, the *Seneca Chief* pulled out of the boat basin at Buffalo Creek. The governor of New York, DeWitt Clinton, and a small army of dignitaries were on board. Great cheers went up from the banks. Cannons boomed along the water all the way to New York City and back again.

The most momentous engineering achievement in the history of the young American republic had been accomplished. The Erie Canal was open for business. The Great Lakes had joined the nation's economic mainstream.

It took eight years, eighty-two locks, and seven million dollars to build, but the canal's effects would be incalculable. Connecting Lake Erie to the Hudson River and from there to the Atlantic, it assured New York's position as chief port and economic center of the country. It brought a land and industrial boom to western New York, furnished a highway for settlement of the Northwest, carried the produce of the new western farmlands inexpensively to the eastern markets, and speeded the development of the Great Lakes.

It also transformed Buffalo from an obscure village to a booming port city, where all these human and material cargos

113

merged. The town was only fourteen years old when canal construction began in 1817. It was not even New York's biggest port on Lake Erie at the time. The distinction belonged to Black Rock, 2 miles up the Niagara River, and when canal construction began, Black Rock expected to be the lake outlet. Buffalo, however, was a little town with big ideas. An energetic and imaginative group of citizens set out to convince the canal commission that Black Rock was a far inferior choice. For one thing, the river bottom was rocky there and ships would find it hard to anchor. It also was a longer trip against the prevailing winds from Black Rock to open water. They followed up their arguments by clearing a sand bar from the mouth of Buffalo Creek and forcing a new channel to the lake. The impressed commission awarded the outlet to Buffalo. Within thirty years it had swallowed up its former rival.

Buffalo's boom picked up steam after the depression of 1837. Grain elevators reshaped the city's skyline. Only Chicago had larger stockyards. Magnificent mansions rose along Delaware Avenue and the other avenues radiating out from Niagara Square. With economic importance came political clout. Two Buffalo residents, Millard Fillmore and Grover Cleveland, became presidents of the United States.

By the turn of the century it was the eighth largest city in America. It became a rival to Cleveland as chief port of the eastern Great Lakes. In an expansive mood it hosted the Pan American Exposition of 1901, a fair best remembered as the site of President McKinley's assassination.

As the century wore on, though, and migration patterns changed, Buffalo's relative size diminished. By the 1980s, it stood only thirty-ninth in population and shared in the national negative reputation of the Lake Erie cities, a reputation that is largely undeserved.

Buffalo undeniably has some of the foulest winter weather in the country. Each year an average of eighty-eight inches of snow falls on the city—and in some winters far more than that. Syracuse is the only big city in America that gets buried deeper. But the same factors that sweep the precipitation in from the lake combine to keep Buffalo pleasantly cool during the summer.

Buffalo is a heavily industrialized city and presents a drab, sooty face to the interstate traffic that whizzes by. Once into the city, though, there are surprising Victorian neighborhoods, a fine concentration of cultural attractions, and prosperous residential areas. Its location at the lakehead is especially dramatic and the lights of the city viewed across miles of open water continue to be a most heartening beacon to Lake Erie mariners.

The area between Buffalo and Erie, is the most scenic on Lake Erie's shore. The final ridge of the Alleghenies approaches to within a few miles of the water here. Rich agricultural lands noted for Concord grape production share the narrow strip with charming towns patterned on New England models. Two of the nineteenth century's most enduring social institutions—the Grange and the Chautauqua—were born in this area and the firm that grew into Welch's Fruit Juices started up in Westfield, New York.

There are vineyard tours just over the Pennsylvania line. That state's tiny chunk of lake frontage, the Erie Triangle, was purchased right after the Revolution from the federal government and several adjacent claimant states. It was a terribly complicated transaction—even the Indians got in on the deal—but worth it to give Pennsylvania a lake port.

Small as this piece of the state may be it is big enough to hold Pennsylvania's third largest city. The city of Erie was an important outpost for the French who built Fort Presque Isle there in 1753. It was taken away by the British, burned down in Pontiac's Rebellion in 1763, and remained abandoned until the Indian threat was ended in the area in 1794. Within twenty years its importance was cemented. Erie was the great U.S. shipyard during the War of 1812. The fleet that swept the British from Lake Erie under Commodore Perry was built there.

Allentown and Teddy Roosevelt

On September 13, 1901, Theodore Roosevelt, vice-president of the United States, was hiking down from the summit of Mt. Marcy in the Adirondacks. As he descended into evening's gathering shadows, he observed a messenger striding rapidly and anxiously toward him. Roosevelt's heart sank. He knew instinctively why the man was there.

Three days before he had left the wounded President William McKinley in Buffalo. McKinley had been gunned down by an assassin while standing in a receiving line at the city's Pan American Exposition on September 6. The vice-president cut short a speaking trip in Vermont and rushed to the president's bedside. But after four days McKinley had improved enormously and doctors assured Roosevelt that the president was out of danger. A much relieved Roosevelt returned to the house in which he had been staying, owned by prominent attorney Ansley Wilcox, on the corner of Delaware and North streets. He planned to join his family in the Adirondacks. Just in case, though, he left a copy of his itinerary with Wilcox. So when he saw the man on the darkening trail three days later he realized there could be only one reason for his being there.

McKinley was dying of gangrene, the result of improperly closed wounds after the operation. By the time Roosevelt reached the train to take him to Buffalo, the president was dead. Arriving in Buffalo on September 14, he went first to pay his respects to the widow. He then returned to the Wilcox house.

Most of McKinley's cabinet was awaiting him in the library. It was decided that Roosevelt must take the oath of office immediately. Borrowing some formal clothes from his host, Roosevelt entered the library at 3:15 P.M. He was sworn in by a U.S. district judge as the twenty-sixth president, the youngest man ever to hold the office at age forty-three and one of the most vigorous executives in the history of the White House.

The Wilcox House, which stands in the midst of the beguiling Allentown district of Buffalo, became a national historic site in 1971, primarily because of its associations with Roosevelt. However, it was something of a landmark even before he took

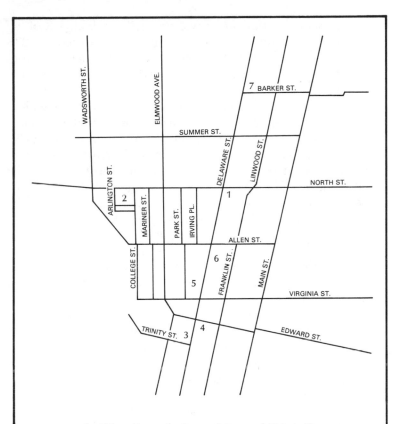

1   Wilcox House, the Roosevelt Inaugural Historic Site
2   Arlington Park
3   Trinity Church
4   Buffalo Club
5   Mark Twain House
6   Horton House
7   Temple Beth Zion

Allentown District of Buffalo

the presidential oath there. It was originally built as part of the officers' headquarters of the Poinsett Barracks, erected in 1838 during a period of friction on the Canadian frontier. The front portion of the present house contained the quarters of commander and post surgeon.

When the army abandoned the post, the house passed into the hands of some of the city's wealthy legal families. Wilcox was given the house as a wedding present in 1884 by his father-in-law. Wilcox's work as a pioneer in civil service reform and social work accustomed him to playing host to nationally important figures when they came through Buffalo. Roosevelt was one of a succession of distinguished house guests. The Wilcoxes occupied the home until their deaths in the early 1930s. It passed out of the family, was used as a restaurant for a time and was scheduled for demolition in the 1960s. But a local citizens' group rescued and restored it and the house was opened to the public on the 70th anniversary of the Roosevelt inauguration.

The National Park Service does its standard excellent job with the home. A ten-minute slide narration explains the history and significance of the Wilcox House. Part of the home has been turned into a museum, recapitulating the dramatic events of September, 1901, in Buffalo. The library and dining room are also open to the public.

The Theodore Roosevelt Inaugural National Historic Site is open Monday to Friday, between 10:00 and 5:00; Saturday and Sunday, noon to 5:00. There is an admission charge.

Delaware Avenue was the most fashionable street in town during the late Victorian years. In the area around the Wilcox House it has retained a great deal of its dignity. The surrounding Allentown area makes for an ideal walk. The fine old homes and apartment houses are now the residences of a younger set, who put on an outdoor art fair every June and patronize the offbeat shops on the side streets. It lacks the commercial ferment of Chicago's Old Town or Toronto's Yorkville—two other Victorian neighborhoods that drew young nostalgists to their streets. But it has retained more of a neighborhood feeling than those other places.

Allentown's approximate boundaries are Virginia to North streets and Franklin to Wadsworth streets, with Delaware Avenue, the main drag, containing many restaurants and cafes. Allen and North streets running east and west are lined with several interesting shops.

The most picturesque of the residential blocks are College Street between Allen and North streets, and Irving Place between the same two streets. Both are beautifully shaded streets with vintage nineteenth-century homes on either side. F. Scott Fitzgerald once lived in the house at 29 Irving Place.

The loveliest part of the district is Arlington Park, just south of the College-North intersection. It is a Londonlike patch of green fronted by some of Allentown's most evocative homes, an unexpected corner of complete charm. Also take a walk down Elmwood Avenue between Allen and Virginia streets. The rows of restored homes, painted in bright pastels, make this one of the most cheerful stretches in the entire city. The oldest home in the city, built by merchant George Coit, is at 412 1/2 Virginia Street. It was constructed in 1813 and was moved to the present site in 1870.

Three blocks south of the Wilcox House on Delaware Avenue is Trinity Episcopal Church, built in 1886 and famous for its Louis Tiffany stained glass windows. Across the street, the Buffalo Club has played an important part in the city's life since its founding in 1867 with Millard Fillmore as initial president. The home of one of its cofounders, William Dorheimer, is on the next block at 434 Delaware Avenue. It was refurbished in 1974. The Katherine Pratt Horton House across the street at 477 Delaware Avenue was built in 1895 and now houses the local headquarters of the Daughters of the American Revolution.

Mark Twain lived for a time at 472 Delaware Avenue as editor and part-owner of the *Express*. The stable at his home is incorporated into the Cloister restaurant. A few blocks farther north is Temple Beth Zion, at 805 Delaware Avenue, one of the most striking ecclesiastical structures in the city with stained glass windows designed by artist Ben Shahn. The temple was completed in 1967 after fire destroyed the original on the same site.

Presque Isle

The first year of the War of 1812 brought nothing but disaster to the American forces around Lake Erie. Detroit fell ignominiously. A relief force was cut to pieces by Indians near Frenchtown (now Monroe), Michigan. The army of General William Henry Harrison was bottled up in western Ohio. The entire southern shore of the lake lay exposed to the British. As the ice melted from Lake Erie in March, 1813, there was only fear of what new calamity the coming spring would bring.

It was very late in the war before the United States understood the necessity of a fleet on Lake Erie if the British were to be contained. Captain Daniel Dobbins, a veteran shipmaster from Pennsylvania, journeyed to the capital himself to plead the case before President Madison. His arguments were so persuasive that he was abruptly given the job of constructing the fleet himself at the isolated port of Erie, which was not quite what Dobbins had in mind. Still he agreed to undertake the task. There were no skilled craftsmen in Erie. Dobbins had to round them up in Pittsburgh and Philadelphia and transport them to this remote outpost. He obtained the services of master carpenter Noah Brown and architect Henry Eckford from New York. He ransacked the Pennsylvania countryside for iron, riggings, and anchors. All the timber had to be cut and squared by hand. Oaks often were cut down in the morning and laid as the keel of a ship by nightfall.

A marker at the foot of Cascade Street, on Erie's west side, marks the site of Dobbins's prolific shipyard. Across the harbor is the sandy, hook-shaped Presque Isle Peninsula, which sheltered the shipyard from the possibility of attack from the lakeside. There was always the threat of a landing down the coast, though, and the town periodically was blockaded by the British fleet under Commodore Barclay.

Oliver Hazard Perry was named commander of the American Lake Erie squadron. When he reached Erie on March 27 there was not a single ship completed. But within fifty-eight days the gunboat *Porcupine,* the schooners *Scorpion* and *Ariel* and the brigs *Lawrence* and *Niagara* would be in the water, an achievement that borders on the impossible.

By mid-July, after the fall of Britain's Fort George in Canada, Perry was able to move five more ships into the lake to join his fleet. He set up recruiting stations throughout the West, offering $10 a month to anyone willing to serve, regardless of experience on water. By the end of the month he had rounded up 300 fighting men, far fewer than the effective fighting force needed for his ten vessels. But his troubles were only beginning. He now had to maneuver his fleet past Presque Isle. The same shallow entrance that had protected his shipyards now presented a formidable obstacle between his fleet and the open water of the lake.

The gunboats made it through in good order. But the two brigs drew nine feet of water and there was only six feet at the sand bar. The *Lawrence,* nonetheless, tried to make it across. It ran aground. Everything movable, including the guns, was taken from the ship, and wooden air chambers, or "camels," were placed on either side to raise her over the sand bar. After two days, the *Lawrence* came free and entered the lake. Now it was the *Niagara's* turn. First its guns were dismounted and placed on shore. It was at this most vulnerable point in the operation that the British fleet suddenly appeared. The *Niagara* was completely out of action. The *Lawrence's* guns were still on shore. But luck had swung over to Perry. It was a rainy, misty day and Barclay, his vision obscured, thought he saw two brigs on the lake and fully armed, ready to engage him. He ordered a retreat. Perry, given all the time he needed, got the *Niagara* dislodged and sailed off in pursuit of Barclay, a pursuit that would end in the destruction of the British fleet off Put-in-Bay, Ohio.

Presque Isle today is a sandy playground, a state park with every imaginable facility available for water recreation. The 7-mile long peninsula contains 3,100 acres. There are eleven beaches along its rim, an ecological reservation and hiking trails in the midst of the mile-wide eastern section, several marinas, and dozens of natural lagoons. A scenic, tree-lined drive follows the outline of the peninsula, opening out on views of the city across the harbor.

Pollution has not been a significant problem in this part of Lake Erie because of the strong offshore currents and deep waters in the area. There is excellent fishing for muskie, pike, bass, and perch in the bay. Experts say, in fact, that the hottest muskie area is at the dock near the site of Daniel Dobbins's shipyards.

The lighthouse near Beach Nine has been revolving its beacon over the lake since 1873. At the southeastern corner of the peninsula is the Perry Victory Monument. Fishermen troll for pike and bass in lagoon waters that reflect the 101-foot-high shaft of Indiana limestone. The monument was erected by the state in 1926 near the spot where Perry was forced to scuttle his fleet during the hard winter following his victory. The privations of that time are memorialized in the name given to the body of water that served as the graveyard of the victorious fleet. To this day it is called Misery Bay.

A quiet lagoon on Presque Isle Peninsula reflects the limestone shaft of the Perry Victory Monument.

A Walk through Erie

Erie is a dignified sort of place by any standard of measurement. Two of its streets in particular—West Sixth and State—have the sort of dignified grace and appearance often found in provincial capitals of Europe. Erie was never quite in that league. But in the mid-nineteenth century, when the canal and later the railroads bore the products of Pittsburgh here for shipping, Erie was a very wealthy port. The wealth that flowed into the town was converted into the splendid structures that stand today along these two streets.

West Sixth Street is lined with impressive homes for about nine blocks, from its intersection with State Street at Perry Square to Cascade Park. That is a bit too far for the purposes of this short walk but if you feel energetic you can try it. A better starting point, however, is the Erie Public Museum, at the corner of Sixth and Chestnut streets.

This mansion was given to the city school district in 1941 for use as a museum and it contains good displays of Erie's colorful past. It is open every day but Monday, 1:00 to 5:00. In July and August it opens at 10:00 on weekdays. There is an admission charge.

Turn up Chestnut Street for one block to West Fifth Street. On the far corner is the former home of Engine Company #4. The old firehouse, built in 1873 and refurbished thirty years later, is now the Firefighters Historical Museum, with almost one thousand items of memorabilia. It is open May through October; Saturday, 10:00 to 5:00 and Sunday, 1:00 to 5:00. There is an admission charge.

Now retrace your steps back to West Sixth and continue to the left. Just down the block is the Erie Art Center, at 338 West Sixth Street built in 1855 by a former medical officer in the U.S. Navy, which explains the cupola in the shape of a ship's wheelhouse. It was occupied by the Morrison family for ninety-one years and Captain William Morrison was the first superintendent of Presque Isle Park. The Art Club of Erie took it over in 1956.

The Church of the Covenant on the next block was built in

1931 and the Presbyterian congregation also owns the adjacent building, a square Victorian edifice erected in 1850. Attorney William S. Lane was the first owner and his brother-in-law lived where the church now stands. You might step inside for a moment to look at the decor of the drawing room and living room on either side of the entrance.

The block between Sassafras and Peach streets may be the most impressive of West Sixth's entire length. On the north side of the street are the Corinthian columns of the Erie County Courthouse. The stately west wing was built in 1855. Next door the order is Ionic on the porch of the Erie Club. The house was built in 1849 by General Charles M. Reed, the city's leading businessman. There is a tradition that he hired unemployed ship carpenters during the slack season to build the interior; as a result it resembles a ship. The Erie Club has occupied the building since 1904.

The impressive St. Paul Episcopal Cathedral, across the street, dates from 1866, and next door to it, at 129 West Sixth Street, is the Hoskinson House with its twin Doric doorways. The Old Main building of Gannon College, right next door, is housed in what was originally the Strong Mansion, built in the 1890s. Gannon held its first classes here in 1944. The school now has a campus of eighteen buildings.

Perry Square, a fine, shaded two-block long park, marks the heart of Erie. Several public buildings, including City Hall and the Metropolitan Library, lie along its margin. To the south, State Street has been turned into a pedestrian mall through the center of the business district. There are fountains and gardens, shops and restaurants along the way, but the centerpiece is the Warner Theatre at the corner of Eighth Street. Built in 1931, this 2,500-seat facility was one of four across the country expressly commissioned by Warner Brothers. It was saved from demolition in the 1970s and serves as a performing arts center. Two blocks to the east is the new Erie Civic Center, a cultural and convention complex with a sports arena, that is the focus of the rebuilt downtown.

Return to Perry Square and continue north on State Street for one block to the city's architectural showpiece, the Custom

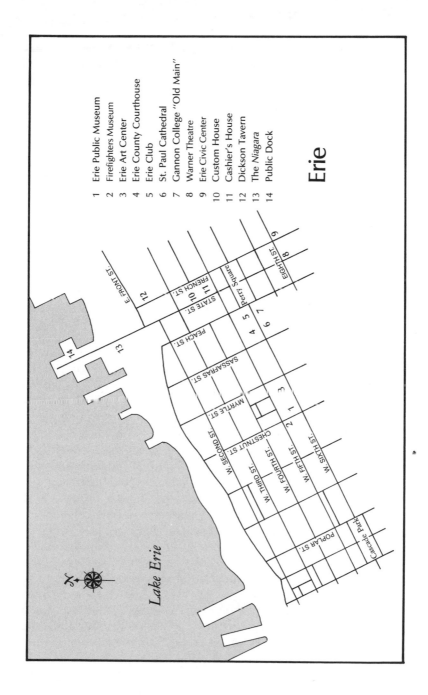

1 Erie Public Museum
2 Firefighters Museum
3 Erie Art Center
4 Erie County Courthouse
5 Erie Club
6 St. Paul Cathedral
7 Gannon College "Old Main"
8 Warner Theatre
9 Erie Civic Center
10 Custom House
11 Cashier's House
12 Dickson Tavern
13 The *Niagara*
14 Public Dock

Erie

House. It is hard to miss; it is the one that looks like a Greek temple. The Custom House supposedly is the first major structure in the country to be built of native stone. Vermont marble was floated here on the Erie Canal to build this early American gem of classic architecture. The style of the columns is Doric.

The Custom House was intended as the Erie branch of the U.S. Bank of Pennsylvania. But when it was completed in 1839 the country was in the middle of a financial depression and within four years the bank failed. The Treasury Department took it over as a customs house for Canadian trade and immigration offices for thirty-nine years until 1888. After various other uses, the Erie County Historical Society acquired it for restoration. Changing displays occupy the main room inside.

Next door is the Cashier's House, built as a dwelling for the bank's chief officer. William Kelly of Philadelphia was the architect for both Greek revival structures. The county historical society now has its offices here and gives guided tours of the house, Tuesday through Saturday, 1:00 to 4:00; also Sunday in June, July, and August.

One block east to French Street is the Dickson Tavern, an early inn that played host to many of the central figures in the great events of 1813. In token of those days it is now called the Commodore Perry Memorial House. Built in 1809, it was the city's leading hotel for many years, entertaining among others the Marquis de Lafayette on his tour of the country in 1825. Later on, it became an important station for the Underground Railroad and scores of escaping slaves were hidden in a series of tunnels and small passages. The city acquired the building in 1924 and several rooms are now restored. It is open from 1:00 to 4:00, but the days it is open vary, so it is best to check in advance. It is generally open weekends all year.

Return to State Street and begin the descent to the water. On the left, risen from its grave in Misery Bay, is Perry's flagship *Niagara*. It was brought up from the depths in 1913 as part of the Perry centennial celebration and has since been restored twice. Much of the wood in the restoration was taken from the original timbers in the keel. It looks today just as it would have appeared before sailing out of the harbor to fight. It is almost comically small. Who today would care to cross the lake in a ship of this size, let alone fight a battle on it? Next to it is the bow of the U.S.S. *Wolverine,* the first ironclad battleship in the United States Navy, built in Erie in 1843, and a veteran of eighty years service on the lakes. The *Niagara* is open 10:00 to 4:30, Tuesday through Saturday; noon to 5:00 on Sunday. There is an admission charge.

State Street ends at the Public Dock. An observation platform looks out over the harbor to the trees of Presque Isle. The shaft of the Perry Monument is clearly visible across the water and the boats sail easily past the end of the peninsula, out into the open lake beyond.

Sightseeing cruises around the harbor and Presque Isle leave hourly from the dock, 10:00 to 9:00, Memorial Day to Labor Day. If you wish to remain landbound, The Buoy, opposite Public Dock, is one of Erie's best seafood restaurants and offers views overlooking the bay.

Other Things to See

[1]   The Albright-Knox Gallery, at the southern edge of Buffalo's lovely Delaware Park, is regarded as one of the outstanding collections of contemporary art in the world. Its galleries contain representatives of every major artistic movement of the last twenty-five years. Its collection of eighteenth-century English portraitists is also first rate. Open Tuesday through Saturday, 11:00 to 5:00; Sunday, noon to 5:00. Donation asked.

[2]   Across Delaware Park Lake is the Buffalo and Erie County Historical Society, the last surviving structure from the Pan American Exposition of 1901. Top exhibits are the turn of the century street and an Erie Canal boat reconstruction. Open Monday through Friday, 10:00 to 5:00; Saturday and Sunday, from noon to 5:00; free.

[3]   The area north of the museum was the site of the Exposition. The Temple of Music, in which McKinley was shot, is long gone but a plaque marks the spot where it stood on Fordham Street, just west of Lincoln Street. After the Exposition closed the area developed into one of the city's most desirable residential neighborhoods.

[4]   On the campus of the State University of New York at Buffalo is the Charles Burchfield Center, at 1300 Elmwood Avenue. It houses works by the water colorist and other artists of Western New York. Tuesday through Saturday, 10:00 to 5:00; Sunday, 1:00 to 5:00; free.

[5]   There is just one piano roll factory still operating in the country and it is at 1026 Niagara Street. The QRS Company continues to produce an enormous library of rolls for devotees of the player piano. Everything from George Gershwin to Liberace is available here, along with hundreds of other selections by less exalted musicians who punched out the tapes for the company. Tours are given twice daily at 10:00 A.M. and 2:00 P.M. on weekdays; at the end of the tour, you can pump one of the pianos yourself.

[6]   The Buffalo Museum of Science, Kensington Expressway at Humboldt Park, displays Chinese ceramics, dinosaur fossils, and just about all the stops in between. Open daily,

10:00 to 5:00; Friday, open to 10:00 P.M., except in July and August; free.

[7]   For a superb view of the skyline, lake, and river, drive through Lasalle Park from the northern or Porter Street entrance.

[8]   Buffalo's major streets radiate out from Niagara Square, the heart of downtown. The granite obelisk dedicated to President McKinley dominates the square. The bulk of City Hall closes off its western end. The twenty-eighth floor observation tower there offers a free panorama of the city. Open Monday through Friday, 9:00 to 3:30. Matched statues of presidents Cleveland and Fillmore flank the building. Both were unveiled in 1932. Fillmore resided the last sixteen years of his life on the site of the Statler-Hilton Hotel across the square. The hotel, by the way, was the first in the nationwide Statler chain and was handsomely restored in the 1970s to regain its position as a Buffalo historic showcase.

[9]   Given the severity of Buffalo's winters, something like the Main Place Mall, at 396 Main Street, was inevitable. It brings the concept of the enclosed suburban shopping plaza right downtown with parking in the same building. Many of the city's major retail stores are located within it, and the city's new light rail system along Main Street brings commuting shoppers right to its front door.

[10]   The Prudential Building is another downtown Buffalo landmark that underwent extensive restoration work in the 1980s. One of the first skyscrapers erected by Louis Sullivan, the building combines the architect's ideas of functional design and ornamentation. It was built in 1896, the same year that Daniel Burnham was finishing his monumental Ellicott Square Building, a few blocks away. At the time it was the largest office building in the world. The Prudential Building, at 28 Church Street, will house the Louis Sullivan Museum when restoration is complete. The Ellicott Square Building, at 295 Main Street, is noted for its mosaic floors.

[11]   The most complete naval military park on the Great Lakes is in Buffalo Harbor. The Naval and Serviceman's Park, on the far side of the New York 5 Freeway from downtown, contains the destroyer USS *The Sullivans* and the guided missile

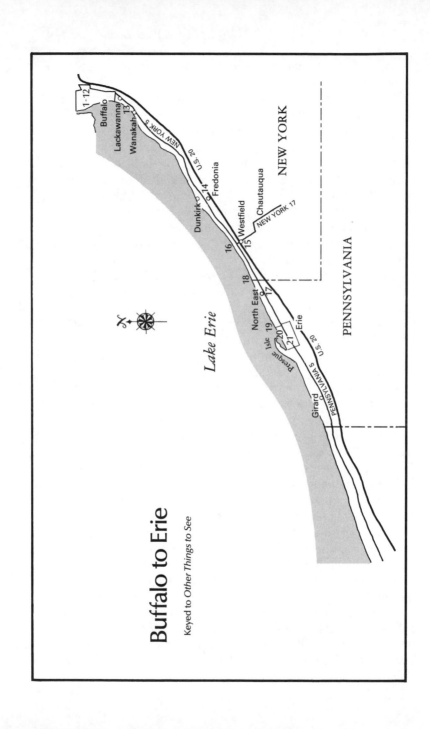

Buffalo to Erie

Keyed to Other Things to See

1-12
Buffalo
Lackawanna
Wanakah
13
NEW YORK 5
U.S. 20
Dunkirk
14
Fredonia
Westfield
Chautauqua
NEW YORK 17
15
16
18
17
North East
Erie
19
20
21
Presque Isle
Girard
PENNSYLVANIA 5
U.S. 20

Lake Erie

NEW YORK

PENNSYLVANIA

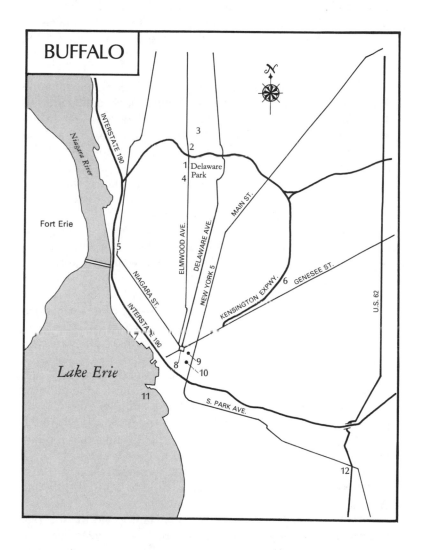

BUFFALO

N

Niagara River

INTERSTATE 190

Fort Erie

Lake Erie

3
2
1 Delaware
4 Park

ELMWOOD AVE.

DELAWARE AVE.

MAIN ST.

NEW YORK 5

5

NIAGARA ST.

INTERSTATE 190

KENSINGTON EXPWY.

GENESEE ST.
6

U.S. 62

7
8
9
10

11

S. PARK AVE.

12

cruiser, USS *Little Rock*. Several other aircraft and weapons from World War II also are on display. The park is open daily, April through November, 10:00 to 6:00. There is an admission charge. Cruises of the harbor also leave the park aboard the *Miss Buffalo* in July and August. Departure times are 12:30 and 3:00.

[12]   The South Park Conservatory on U.S. 62 (South Park) has sixteen greenhouses of exotic plants. Open daily, 9:00 to 4:00; free. Just south of the Park, in Lackawanna, the white marble towers of Our Lady of Victory Basilica are a local landmark. Visitors are welcome to see the interior, daily, 6:30 A.M. to 9:00 P.M.

[13]   Lake Shore Drive west of the city affords interesting views of the Buffalo skyline, of Canada's Point Abino, and of the stately homes of Buffalo suburbanites.

[14]   Fredonia, New York, a town with a pronounced New England air to it, has memorials to the first grange and the first chapter of the Women's Christian Temperance Union on its town square. A branch of the State University of New York contributes to this ambience, while the Barker Library Museum displays the high points in the town's lively history. It is open Monday, Tuesday, and Thursday, 10:00 to 9:00; Wednesday, Friday, and Saturday, 10:00 to 5:00. There is no admission charge.

[15]   The Concord grape is king around these parts and Westfield, New York, pays homage to it with a vine-adorned monument in the town square. Buildings used by Welch's, the grape juice people, are right across the street. This is where the firm began. Also on the square is the Chautauqua County History Center and Museum, housed in the McClurg Mansion. Open May through October, Tuesday through Saturday, 10:00 to 12:00 and 1:00 to 4:00; Sunday, 2:00 to 5:00, in July and August; admission charge.

[16]   The lighthouse in Barcelona Harbor was the first one to be lit by natural gas. That was in 1828, seven years after the first gas well in America was dug in nearby Fredonia, New York. There is a good view of the bluffs along the lakeshore from the old light.

[17]   North East is the center of Pennsylvania's Concord grape country. Winery tours are offered daily during the summer at the Penn-Shore Winery, 10225 East Lake Road, and Mazza Vineyards, 11815 East Lake Road.

[**18**]   Highway 5, between Dunkirk, New York, and Erie, Pennsylvania, is the most scenic in the area. There are fine lake views to the north with forested hills and vineyards to the south.

[19]   "You may fire when ready, Gridley," said Admiral Dewey at the start of the Battle of Manila Bay in 1898. Unfortunately for the Spanish fleet, Captain Charles Gridley was ready. He commanded Dewey's flagship, *Olympia,* and lies buried in Lakeside Cemetery on Erie's east side. The grave is guarded by a Spanish cannon from Manila.

[20]   The first lighthouse on the Great Lakes was constructed just east of the foot of Dunn Boulevard in 1818. It is not the one that stands there now, however. This lighthouse was built in 1866, the third on the same spot, and retired nineteen years later. There is a nice view over the harbor to Presque Isle from the heights.

[21]   General Anthony Wayne was on his way home to Philadelphia in 1796 after his brilliant campaign against the Indians in the west. But he only made it as far as Erie. He died in a blockhouse which stood on what is now the grounds of the State Soldier-Sailor home on East Third and Ash streets. He was buried there for a time but his son later removed the body to Radnor. A replica of the blockhouse was built in 1880. It is behind the home and across a railroad footbridge. Open Memorial Day to Labor Day. There is no admission charge.

Side Trips

There are several ski areas southeast of Buffalo along U.S. 219. The closest to the city is Kissing Bridge, about 35 miles south on N.Y. 240, near East Aurora. That town was also the home of Millard Fillmore in the years when the thirteenth President of the United States was starting up his law practice. His house, at 24 Shearer Avenue, is now a museum. It is open Monday, Wednesday, and Sunday in summer, 2:30 to 4:30. There is an admission charge.

A 15-mile steam railroad excursion leaves from Arcade, 44 miles southeast of Buffalo, on the Arcade and Attica Railroad. It operates on weekends, Memorial Day to October. During July and August a Wednesday trip is added. Check locally for times and fares.

In Batavia, 39 miles east of Buffalo, the Holland Purchase Museum was originally the land office of the company that opened up this portion of New York. It was built in 1815. Open Monday through Saturday, between 10:00 and 5:00; Sunday, 2:00 to 5:00; free.

That fabled instrument of educational uplift, the Chautauqua, is still going strong into its second century. It was founded in 1874 on Chautauqua Lake, 11 miles southeast of Westfield, and sent traveling shows to spread culture around the country in the age before movies, television, and long-playing records. It still offers two months of programs during the summer. Admission is charged to the grounds; concerts and recitals require an added fee. The institution also offers yacht trips around the lake in summer, except on Monday, at 2:00 P.M. and 3:30 P.M. Added 7:00 P.M. trips on weekends and Wednesdays.

Waterford, Pennsylvania, 16 miles south of Erie on U.S. 19 is the site of Fort Le Boeuf. It was built by the French in 1753 over English objections, which were delivered personally by the young George Washington. There is a museum and a restored home, the Judson House, dating from 1820, on the site of the fort. Remains of later American fortifications also are visible. Open Tuesday through Saturday, 9:00 to 4:30; Sunday from 1:00 to 4:30. There is an admission charge.

The first commercial oil well in the United States, the Drake Well, opened in Titusville in 1859. The town, 46 miles south of Erie, has a replica of the well and a museum of oil. Open Tuesday through Saturday, 9:00 to 4:30; Sunday from noon; admission charge.

State Parks on the Lake

Access to the facilities of two state parks is available from Dunkirk, New York. Lake Erie State Park, 7 miles west, has a beach, rental cabins, and 95 campsites. Evangola, 17 miles east, has a 4,000-foot sand beach, a cafe, a game terrace, and 51 campsites.

If you go for a weekend: Stay in Buffalo.

1. Explore the downtown area around Niagara Square, take the afternoon tour through the QRS Piano Roll plant.

2. See the Wilcox House and take the Allentown walk outlined in this chapter.

3. Visit some of the city's excellent museums: the Albright-Knox, the Historical Society, and the Museum of Science.

If you go for a week: Stay in Buffalo three nights, in Westfield for one night, and in Erie for three nights.

1–3. Same as the weekend tour.

4. Spend the night in Westfield and visit nearby Chautauqua for a concert, play, or lecture.

5. Continue along scenic Highway 5 to Erie. Take the downtown walk outlined in this chapter.

6. Spend the day on Presque Isle.

7. Take the side trip to Fort Le Boeuf and the oilfields around Titusville.

The most far-ranging view of Cleveland is available from the observation deck of the Terminal Tower on Public Square.

6

Cleveland and the Western Reserve

Connecticut owned the land first. In the years following the American Revolution, when other states surrendered their claims in the West to form the Northwest Territory, Connecticut held on to this tract. It was to be a Western Reserve, new land for those in the state who had been burned out and impoverished by the war.

The reserve extended from the Pennsylvania border to Sandusky Bay. This enormous chunk of territory remained virtually deserted until 1794 when the Battle of Fallen Timbers ended the Indian threat to northern Ohio. Then from the East the dispossessed and restless came pouring into the promising new region.

The settlements they created in the lakeshore forests were built on New England models. A few of them—Norwalk, Hambden, Windsor—were even named for the settlers' hometowns in Connecticut. Many of the smaller communities have preserved some of their New England aura. Even in Cleveland, tumultuous Public Square retains vestiges amid the skyscrapers of the grassy New England commons it used to be.

Cleveland generally would be the last place anyone would associate with the pleasant villages of the Northeast. It has been the butt of jokes for years, held up as the great American example of megalopolis running amok. Its lakefront was an environmental horror story. It became the first American city since the Great Depression to default on its debts. Even its river, the Cuyahoga, caught fire one surreal afternoon. Some of its more disenchanted residents took to calling it the "Mistake on the Lake."

For all its besmirched reputation, though, Cleveland can keep a visitor pleasantly occupied for days, and will even sneak in a few surprises if one is not careful. A book by one of its admirers, in fact, describes the city as "the best kept secret."

It boasts a collection of museums that is one of the country's most impressive and diverse. Its rapid transit system is excellent. Its downtown has sewn new projects into its fabric while preserving the best of its past. A lively interest in the city's roots has arisen in recent years. Projects anchored in the past have developed downtown in Playhouse Square, in Ohio City on the west bank of the river, even at Settler's Landing where the pioneering party led by Moses Cleaveland came ashore in 1796.

Most of the major cities in the Reserve were settled in the generation after Fallen Timbers. Cleveland was only one of several thriving towns of approximately equal size and importance. Painesville and Fairport rivalled it as lake outlets. Sandusky and Vermilion surpassed it in economic importance. Huron and Mentor considered themselves its equal. As the nation moved westward and the paths of commerce converged upon Lake Erie, one of these towns was bound to become a fabulously wealthy metropolis. But it was not until 1827 that Cleveland was assured of that role.

The town was then still a small collection of cabins when the state legislature chose its harbor for the terminus of the new Ohio and Lake Erie Canal. Just as the choice of Buffalo as the outlet of the Erie Canal in New York made it the metropolis of the eastern lake, Cleveland's selection as Ohio's canal port created the impetus that made it the largest city of the central lake.

It was in the decades following the Civil War that the city

was transformed. It became the focus of Great Lakes shipbuilding, with giants like Alva Bradley transferring their operations here. Cleveland ships and capital developed the iron and copper mines of northern Michigan and Minnesota. The ore was brought back to the city and shaped in giant industrial complexes with coal that came up the canal from the vast fields of nearby West Virginia.

Oil was discovered in Pennsylvania, and Cleveland became the country's first refining center. This is where the Rockefeller fortune was founded. Incredible wealth poured into the city. Euclid Avenue east of downtown was lined with mansions, supposedly the richest street in America. With economic power came political clout and Ohio men bankrolled from Cleveland controlled national Republican politics for years. James Garfield of Mentor became president and industrialist Mark Hanna put his friend William McKinley in the White House, too.

The tycoons cared about their city. They built skyscrapers downtown and left their enormous estates to be used as city parks. Cleveland built the tallest office building outside Manhattan Island, the largest city-owned stadium in the country. Even into the 1920s it was regarded as Chicago's leading rival as the financial center of the Midwest. When young Henry Luce started *Time* magazine he moved its operations for a while to Cleveland, in the belief that he would be closer to the pulse of the nation's commerce than in New York.

Cleveland reached a peak population of more than 900,000 in 1950, the country's seventh largest city. Since then it has lost 350,000 people, although its metropolitan area remains the nineteenth largest in the country. The city's suburbs are expansive and affluent, particularly around the long established Shaker Heights area in the east and along the lakeshore on the west. In addition to a lot of people, the suburbs have taken the city's basketball team and a good deal of its cultural activity away from the downtown area.

But much abides. Cleveland's wealth of ethnic diversity, although no longer patterned into tight neighborhoods, still shapes the city's personality. It trails only New York and Chicago as a corporate headquarters. The University Circle district on the east side is one of the nation's most impressive concentrations of museums and educational facilities. New downtown projects are making fine use of air and open space, reminiscent of the original plans of the settlers for Public Square.

Cleveland still hears the jokes. It can even laugh at some of them. More importantly, the city is doing something about its image and cleaning up the mess that fed all the hilarity. The mistake on the lake is slowly being corrected.

Square, Mall, and Arcade in Cleveland

Any stroll through downtown Cleveland must begin in Public Square. The ten-acre meadow appears on the earliest maps of the city. In the minds of Cleveland's New England founders it was the focus of the new settlement, and it has remained there through the intervening years, although the grass long ago turned to concrete.

The square is bisected on the east-west axis by Superior Avenue and on the north-south line by Ontario Street. The intersection is the city's geographic dividing line. Originally, the streets stopped at the square and traffic wound lazily around its perimeter. But by 1867 Cleveland had become such a busy place that bucolic luxuries could no longer be afforded. Down came the restraining fence and in came the traffic. A bus terminal has grabbed off one of its corners, as well.

Four major structures, each one reflecting a bit of the city's history, make up the interior of Public Square—two statues and two memorials. In the southwestern corner stands a statue of Moses Cleaveland, the city's founder. He led the group of original settlers into the area in 1796, stayed for four months, went home to Connecticut, and never came back again. His name had staying power, though, even if the first "a" was dropped by the mid-nineteenth century. The popular legend is that a newspaper printer, pressed for space in his masthead, invented the abbreviated version. The life-sized, bronze statue has stood here since 1888.

Just to the north of Cleaveland is a seated Tom L. Johnson, the city's mayor from 1901 to 1909. In the minds of many he was the most gifted man ever to occupy the spot. Although a millionaire, he was also a reformer and a champion of the working classes. He left his mark on the city in the nearby Mall, a project he felt was the capstone of his public career.

To the east of Johnson's statue is the Light of Friendship, a gift to the city from General Electric, commemorating the fact that this was the first square in the world to be illuminated by electricity. The lights came on in 1879. Rounding out the square grouping is the Soldiers and Sailors Monument, a 125-foot shaft topped by a statue of liberty. Inside, the names of Cuyahoga County men who served in the Civil War are engraved on marble panels. The monument has been here since 1894, displacing an earlier memorial to Commodore Perry which was moved elsewhere in the city. So it goes with war heroes.

Dominating the square is the Terminal Tower, the 708-foot high wedding cake that for thirty years held the distinction of being the tallest building in the world outside Manhattan. The forty-second-floor observatory is open daily from 8:45 to 4:45; admission charge.

The tower, opened in 1929, was the project of the Van Sweringen brothers, the crown of a rail and real estate empire that shaped much of modern Cleveland. The twin brothers developed Shaker Heights as a leafy suburb for the upper crust. To enable its residents to speed to work downtown, the brothers then purchased the Nickel Plate Railroad and turned it into a commuter line. Its terminal was at Public Square. At that time, the area southwest of the square was a squalid, decaying section of town. Nevertheless, the Van Sweringens managed to get the site of the city's new railroad station, originally intended for the Mall, switched to a site adjacent to their little commuter terminal. Up went the tower to celebrate and house the complex. Public Square which had slipped steadily from the center of activity was once again installed at Cleveland's heart. Standard Oil has returned to the heart of the city of its birth, and its massive office complex on the southeastern corner of the square is scheduled for completion in the mid-1980s.

On the northern end of the square, at Ontario and Rockwell streets, is the Old Stone Church, with its entrance around the corner on Ontario Street. The First Presbyterian Church was built here in 1834 and the current building dates from twenty-one years later. The interior, graced by several exquisite Tiffany windows and deep wood paneling, is a welcome oasis from the commotion outside.

One block east along Rockwell Avenue is the head of the Mall, a great rectangular park bounded by public buildings and dappled with fountains. It extends north for two blocks, opening up onto Lake Erie with views of the water and of Cleveland

1   Terminal Tower
2   Standard Oil Building
3   Old Stone Church
4   Cleveland Stadium
5   War Memorial Fountain
6   Old Federal Building
7   City Hall
8   New Federal Building
9   Ohio Bell Building
10 Erieview Plaza
11 Medical Mutual Building
12 St. John Cathedral
13 Cleveland Trust Building
14 The Old Arcade
15 Inn on the Square

Downtown Cleveland

Stadium, the massive home of baseball's Indians and football's Browns.

The War Memorial Fountain, added to the Mall in a 1964 facelift, is one of the city's most popular lunchtime assembly points. On a spring afternoon the entire area is among the most enticing urban scenes anywhere, with strollers, brown-baggers and fountain-fanciers making a congenial jumble of humanity. Inspired by the heroic architecture of the Columbian Exposition of 1893, the forty-acre Mall was Mayor Johnson's proudest achievement. The old Federal Building on Rockwell Avenue is its oldest structure. The city library, city hall, board of education building, county courthouse, and convention center rounded out the grouping over the years.

After admiring the waterscape from the Lakeside Avenue end of the Mall, walk east to Sixth Street and City Hall. Displayed inside is the painting *The Spirit of '76*, rendered by Clevelander Archibald Willard for the centennial celebration. The city claims that this is the first version of the often-copied work. To clinch the case, Cleveland named the park next door after Willard.

Across Lakeside Avenue is the new Federal Building, completed in 1967 and typical of the new look in downtown Cleveland. Further evidence lies around the corner on Ninth Street. This thoroughfare has become a showcase for some of the most striking architecture in the city. At the corner of Lakeside Avenue is the Ohio Bell Building, and next to it, the tree-lined plaza of the Erieview complex. The large open space gives a feeling of airiness to what easily could have become a dark downtown canyon. Across St. Clair Avenue is the Medical Mutual Building, whose bold outline has become the most visible symbol of the renewed central city. The Gothic structure on the next block on Ninth Street is St. John Cathedral, with still more open space in its huge plaza.

One block ahead on the right but much lower on the spiritual scale is Short Vincent Street. Actually, its true name is Vincent Avenue, but Clevelanders who patronized its curving, block-long row of saloons referred to it in the affectionate diminutive. Short Vincent Street has lost much of its steam in recent years. With the exception of the venerable Theatrical Restaurant, most of its abbreviated length has been given over to somber parking structures.

Across Euclid Avenue and on the left is the Cleveland Trust Building. Step into the lobby for a few minutes and look up at the eighty-five-foot high Tiffany glass dome, completed in 1908. An even more arresting example of vintage Cleveland architecture lies a few blocks west along Euclid Avenue to the right. The Old Arcade, at 401 Euclid, opened in 1890, is one of the most charming relics of the Victorian age surviving in any major American city. The glass-roofed, 400-foot long structure connecting Euclid and Superior avenues contains 112 shops in its five levels, a strange and distant echo of the most contemporary style of suburban shopping malls. Many of the stores have been turned into an astonishing assortment of fast-food restaurants, and tables have been placed along the balcony rail to accommodate the lunchtime carry-out trade. With the banner-decked interior splashing color all around, it makes for one of the cheeriest spots in town.

For a more formal repast, and a fitting conclusion to this stroll, go back to Euclid Avenue and walk across the width of Public Square to the handsomely restored Inn on the Square. The locally-based Stouffer's Corporation took a deteriorating commercial property and did a fine job of renovation. The main lobby with its massive chandelier is especially attractive, and a variety of restaurants are open in the hotel.

University Circle

Cleveland was the place to put together a fortune in the last decades of the nineteenth century. It did not take a Rockefeller to do it, either. He was just one of many who grew with the city. One such man was Jeptha H. Wade, whose crowning achievement was the assembling of the Western Union Telegraph Company. Upon his death in 1882 he willed the city a large forested tract on the east side, which was gratefully accepted and named Wade Park. It was from this land that the city's University Circle area was shaped.

University Circle, extending east of the intersection of Euclid and East Boulevard, now encompasses 500 acres. The city's major museums are concentrated here, along with its largest assemblage of medical, cultural, religious, and educational facilities. The three great museums of art, history, and natural history dominate the parklike circle. Close by are the Garden Center of Greater Cleveland, Severance Hall (home of the Cleveland Orchestra), the Cleveland Medical Museum, the institutes of music and art, and the university that gives the area its name, Case Western Reserve.

At one time the two schools, Case and Western, were separate and very competitive institutions, reflective of the rivalry that existed between the families that sponsored them. Case was started as a technical school by an old Cleveland family that had become rich in real estate. Railroad tycoon Amasa Stone then saw the chance to one-up the Cases. He offered tiny Western Reserve College $500,000 if it would move from the village of Hudson to a Cleveland location right next door to Case. That understandably led to some friction; but since their merger in 1967, the two schools have blended almost totally.

The universities were the magnet for the other cultural attractions in the area. At least two days can be spent examining their treasures. Start at the Cleveland Museum of Art, separated from Euclid Avenue by gardens and a reflecting pool. The neo-classic structure, opened in 1916, and the connecting building which was opened forty-one years later, contain one of the largest, most diverse collections in the country. Its bequest list reads like a roll call of Cleveland's great families. The Severances, who also funded nearby Severance Hall, were responsible for the armor court and the tapestries that adorn it. The Holdens, former publishers of the *Cleveland Plain Dealer,* contributed an outstanding collection of Italian primitives. The grand-nephew of Senator Mark Hanna left a $20 million endowment and a collection valued at $1.4 million in 1957. Open Tuesday through Friday, from 10:00 to 6:00; Wednesday to 10:00; Saturday, 9:00 to 5:00; Sunday, 1:00 to 6:00; free.

Around the circle to the left is the Cleveland Museum of Natural History—another Case family project—which opened at this site in 1958. Exhibits include Ohio's only dinosaur, a planetarium, ecology, mammals, prehistoric Cleveland, butterflies, and the complete range of the natural sciences. Open Monday through Saturday, 10:00 to 5:00; Sunday, 1:00 to 5:30. There is an admission charge.

The third great museum on the circle is the Western Reserve Historical Society Museum, housed in two turn-of-the-century mansions. An exhibit area and library bridging the space between the two homes was completed in 1959. The museum contains excellent exhibits relating to the history of Cleveland and the Western Reserve, the development of American decorative arts, the Shakers, and the hemisphere's largest collection of items relating to Napoleon. Attached to it is the Frederick C. Crawford Auto-Aviation Museum, recalling Cleveland's position at the center of the automotive industry in its earliest years. Open Tuesday through Saturday, from 10:00 to 5:00; Sunday, 2:00 to 5:00; admission charge.

Other museums in the immediate area are:

The Garden Center of Greater Cleveland, at 11030 East Boulevard, with horticultural displays and herb, rose, and Japanese gardens. Open Monday through Friday, 9:00 to 5:00; Sunday, 2:00 to 5:00; free.

The Howard Dittrick Museum of Historical Medicine, at 11000 Euclid, contains exhibits on the development of medical techniques and instruments and changing concepts about the treatment of illness. Open Monday through Friday, 10:00 to 5:00; Sunday, 1:00 to 5:00. In June, July, and August closed Sunday, open Saturday, 1:00 to 5:00; free.

The Garfields of Mentor

Seven Ohioans have become presidents of the United States, though none was especially successful at the job. Grant and Harding were surrounded by some of the more venal politicians in American history. Hayes was voted in amid some of the murkiest dealings in electoral lore. Taft and Benjamin Harrison were rejected by the voters after a single term. McKinley and Garfield were assassinated.

James A. Garfield was in office only four months when he was shot down in a Washington railroad station in July, 1881. In spite of his doctors' best efforts, he almost recovered. But the combination of medical incompetence and two months of pain were too much for even his robust frame and he succumbed in September of that year.

Garfield had been regarded as Cleveland's president. He was born in eastern Cuyahoga County and worked as a young man on the Ohio and Lake Erie Canal. He was educated at nearby Hiram College, later becoming its president. He rose to major-general in a distinguished Civil War career and entered Congress in 1863 as a radical Republican.

Garfield was elected to the Senate by the Ohio legislature in 1880 but before he could take his seat he was also chosen as the Republican presidential nominee as a compromise candidate. It was, however, an ineffective compromise. The aftermath of the convention caused a deep and bitter split in the party and Garfield was shot by a disappointed office seeker who claimed to be a supporter of the Grant faction.

Before his election, Garfield had moved to Lawnfield, a rambling old home in the town of Mentor, about 22 miles northeast of Public Square. On the north side of U.S. 20, at 8095 Mentor Avenue, the house preserves the Garfield family's original furnishings along with the president's books, desk, and campaign and personal memorabilia. Garfield carried on the country's first front porch campaign for the office, receiving delegations at home rather than traveling among the electorate. The front porch he used was Lawnfield's. He was also the last president who was born in a log cabin and a replica of his birthplace is on the grounds, along with his campaign office.

Garfield lay in state in Public Square for two days before his burial in Lakeview Cemetery, at Euclid Avenue and East 123rd Street in Cleveland. A 180-foot high monument to him was opened there nine years after his death in one of the cemetery's most scenic corners. It is on a rise that overlooks the lake and also commands a view of the city's distant towers. He was subsequently joined at Lakeview by Mark Hanna who began his rise to national political prominence by working in Garfield's campaign. Also at Lakeview, is another prominent Clevelander who chose to come back home at the end, John D. Rockefeller.

Lawnfield is open May through October, Tuesday through Saturday, 9:00 to 5:00; Sunday, 1:00 to 5:00. There is an admission charge.

Other Things to See

[1]   The Conneaut Historical Railroad Museum, in the industrial port that lies just inside the Pennsylvania border, is located in the former New York Central depot. The address is 324 Depot Street, but signs throughout the town give directions. It is open between Memorial Day and Labor Day, noon to 5:00; free.

[2]   The flavor of the old lake port of Ashtabula comes alive on Bridge Street, which has become an attractive row of antique stores, restaurants, and places of entertainment. It is located just west of the Ashtabula River bridge and overlooks the harbor, marina, and enormous coal-loading dock in one of northeastern Ohio's liveliest settings.

[3]   Pioneer Robert Harper built Shandy Hall in 1815 and his family occupied the frame structure for the next 120 years. Preserved within it is an astonishing collection of articles used by the Harpers over all the years they occupied the home. Apparently they never threw anything away. Furniture, toys, tools, silverware, portraits—all here, binding the years together in a web of family continuity. On one parlor wall is the portrait of one of the Harper women who had posed in a shawl. Draped on a chair below the portrait is the very shawl. The home is named for the novel *Tristam Shandy,* a favorite of the builder's daughter. Shandy Hall is located on Ohio 84, just east of Unionville and south of Geneva. It is operated by the Western Reserve Historical Society. A fee is charged for the excellent guided tour. Open May through October, Tuesday through Saturday, 10:00 to 5:00; Sunday, between 1:00 and 5:00.

[4]   Fairport was once the busiest lake harbor in Ohio. Now it is a drowsy town, just north of Painesville, with a decided New England air to it. A marine museum, housed partially in an old lighthouse and pilot house atop a lakeside bluff, recalls its glory days. Open Memorial Day to Labor Day, weekends and holidays, from 1:00 to 6:00; admission charge.

[5]   The Holden Arboretum, five miles southeast of Mentor on Sperry Road, has one of the world's largest collections of wood plants. Among the top attractions in its 2,600 acres and 6,000 varieties are ornamental trees, azaleas, maples, and

viburnums. The rolling landscape accentuates the beauty of the exhibits. There are also nature trails and more demanding hiking routes. Open Tuesday through Sunday; April through October, 10:00 to 7:00; rest of year, from 10:00 to 4:00; admission charge.

[6]   The Kirtland Temple was the first house of worship built by the Mormons, opening in 1836 after three years of construction and built to the specifications of Joseph Smith, Jr., founder of the Church of the Latter Day Saints. Powerful in its dignified simplicity, the temple has held up well over the years and is owned today by the Reorganized Church, which is headquartered in Independence, Missouri. It is open in summer, 9:00 to 7:00; on Sunday, 1:00 to 5:00. In the rest of the year, the weekday hours are 9:00 to 5:00. There is no admission charge, guide service is provided, and a small museum adjoins the temple.

[7]   The Cleveland Health Museum, first such facility in the country, features displays explaining the functions of the human body and how disease and illness can be prevented. It is located at 8911 Euclid Avenue. Open Tuesday through Saturday, 9:00 to 4:30; Sunday, 1:00 to 4:30; admission charge.

[8]   One of the more striking tributes to Cleveland's ethnic diversity is the Cultural Gardens in Rockefeller Park. Seventeen nationalities are represented in the chain of blooms and statues along East and Liberty boulevards between St. Clair and Superior avenues. Busts of famous men are placed amid trees, lawns, and flowers to celebrate the city's cultural makeup. Other gardens in the area are dedicated to peace, brotherhood, and Shakespeare.

[9]   Rockefeller Park also contains greenhouses with a Japanese garden and a garden for the blind. They are at 750 East 88th Street, just north of St. Clair Avenue.

[10]   As Cleveland was growing the Dunham family ran a tavern and inn on the old stagecoach road to Buffalo and the East. From 1824 to 1857 it was a major social center for the young city. Now the Dunham Tavern Museum recreates the ambience of that period amid the clatter and congestion of the city's east side. Located at 6709 Euclid Avenue, the old tavern—

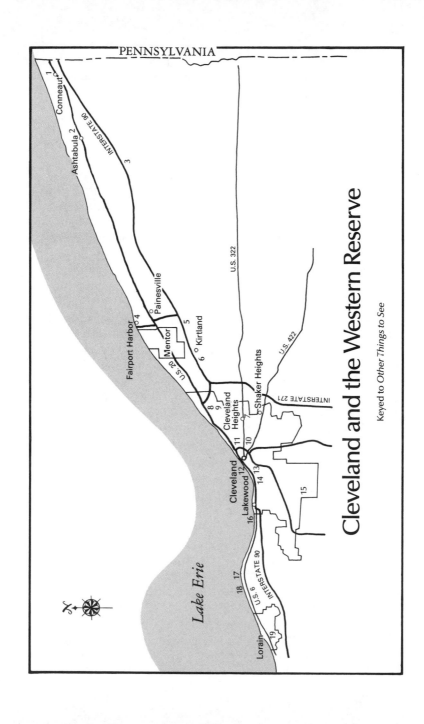

PENNSYLVANIA

Cleveland and the Western Reserve

Keyed to Other Things to See

Lake Erie

Conneaut 1
Ashtabula 2
INTERSTATE 90
3
U.S. 322
U.S. 422
Painesville
Fairport Harbor
4
5
Kirtland 6
Mentor
U.S. 20
6
INTERSTATE 271
Shaker Heights
8
9
Cleveland Heights
11
10
12
Cleveland
13
Lakewood
14
16
15
18 17
U.S. 6
INTERSTATE 90
19
Lorain

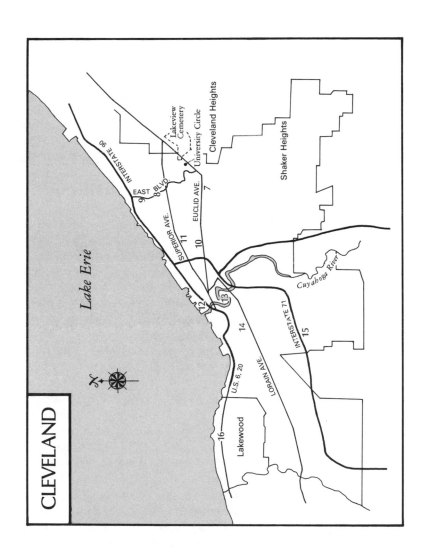

CLEVELAND

Lake Erie

INTERSTATE 90

EAST BLVD.
9
8

SUPERIOR AVE.
11

EUCLID AVE.
7

10

Lakeview
Cemetery

University Circle

Cleveland Heights

Shaker Heights

12

13

14

Cuyahoga River

INTERSTATE 71
15

U.S. 6, 20

LORAIN AVE.

16

Lakewood

which subsequently had become an architect's office, a private residence, and a tearoom—is one of the Western Reserve's most historic buildings. In 1941 it was restored to the appearance of its heyday. Especially intriguing is the atmospheric old taproom, with original floor and tables. Open Tuesday through Sunday, 12:30 to 4:30; admission charge.

[11]   There used to be a ballpark at Lexington and 66th Street. As a matter of fact, there still is. League Park, once the home of the Cleveland Indians baseball team, is now a public recreation field, and a portion of the third base grandstand still stands as a tribute to the past. The park was the scene of the pitching exploits of Cy Young in the 1890s and the heroics of Nap Lajoie in the following decade. It was permanently replaced as the home of the Indians by the lakefront stadium after World War II.

[12]   The Goodtime Cruise Line operates excursions down the fiery Cuyahoga and around Lake Erie and harbor areas, daily except Monday, from May 3 to Labor Day. Between June 15 and the end of the season, five daily trips are given aboard the 500-passenger, diesel-powered boat from the East Ninth Street Pier. Inquire locally for times and rates. Also on the pier is the USS *Cod*, a perfectly preserved World War II submarine credited with sinking 30,000 tons of enemy shipping in the Pacific. It is open Memorial Day to Labor Day, weekdays, 11:00 to 4:00; weekends, 1:00 to 5:00. There is an admission charge.

[13]   The Flats is the area on Cleveland's near west side that lies at river level. It is not immediately apparent that the city sits on a bluff until one ventures down to Settler's Landing, where the Moses Cleaveland party first came ashore, and looks up at downtown Cleveland far above on the heights. The area of winding streets that follow the Cuyahoga River's contours, between industry and bridge abutments, is one of Cleveland's most interesting corners, with restaurants and night spots tucked away here and there. A plaque below the Superior Avenue bridge marks Cleaveland's Landing and another marker commemorates the log cabin of Lorenzo Carter, who stayed on to run a trading post and tavern here and keep the settlement going long after Cleaveland went home to Connecticut.

[14]   Ohio City, once a great rival to Cleveland on the western bank of the Cuyahoga River, is now a part of the city marked by its ethnic variety. Lorain Avenue (Ohio 10), the main street, is filled with European restaurants, predominantly Hungarian and Slavic. Antique dealers have clustered along its length, too, and on the nearby side streets young couples looking for bargains in urban living have purchased and restored the area's aging but immaculate houses. Ohio City residents once burned down the bridge across the Cuyahoga that linked it to Cleveland and a pitched battle between the two towns was narrowly averted in the early nineteenth century. It was swallowed up by the larger city in 1857. Focus of its activity is the West Side Market, Lorain Avenue at 25th Street, where the ethnic mix comes together in all its bubbling zest.

[15]   The Metroparks Zoological Park is in Brookside Park off Interstate 71 in the Cleveland area's southwestern section. There are 1,100 animals displayed on 125 attractively landscaped acres. Open daily, 9:00 to 5:00; Sunday and holidays, April to October, 9:00 to 7:00. There is an admission charge.

[16]   The Old Stone House in Lakewood, 6 miles west of downtown Cleveland, preserves a home built in 1838. It is furnished as a typical pioneer home of the era would have appeared. Open Wednesday and Sunday, 2:00 to 5:00; closed December and January; admission charge.

[17]   U.S. 6 between the Cleveland city limits and Lorain, Ohio, is a very attractive drive, winding through some of the area's finest residential suburbs and opening out on occasional views of the lake.

[18]   A large chunk of scenic Lake Erie shoreline is preserved for public use in Bay Village along U.S. 6 in Metropark Huntington. The park also contains a nature and science center with live animals and a marine tank. It is open daily, except Wednesday, 1:00 to 5:00. There is no admission charge.

[19]   Lorain's Lakeview Park on U.S. 6 is a dandy place for a picnic among the rose gardens, fountains, and recreational facilities. There are views of Lake Erie, harbor, and the world's second largest bascule bridge, operated on the principle of counter-balanced weights.

Side Trips

In Akron, 33 miles south of Cleveland, is Stan Hywet Hall and Gardens, a Tudor mansion filled with art treasures by rubber magnate F. A. Seiberling. Open daily except Monday. There is an admission charge.

In Bath, 23 miles south-southeast of Cleveland, is the Hale Farm and Village, a Western Reserve Historical Society restoration of a nineteenth-century agricultural settlement built around an 1826 brick farmhouse. Open May through October and December; Tuesday through Saturday, 10:00 to 5:00; Sunday, noon to 6:00. Admission charge.

In Aurora, 23 miles southeast of Cleveland, is Sea World, a seventy-acre park with marine exhibits and amusements built around a nautical theme. Open Memorial Day to mid-September, 9:00 A.M. to 10:00 P.M.; admission charge.

In Welshfield, 29 miles southeast of Cleveland, is the Welshfield Inn, built in 1842 and once an Underground Railway stop. It still serves meals, except on Monday, and takes in a few overnight guests. A few miles north, in Burton, the Geauga County Historical Museum and Century Village recreates a crossroads village of Ohio's pioneer days. Open May through October, Tuesday through Saturday, 10:00 to 5:00; Sunday, 1:00 to 5:00; admission charge.

In Oberlin, 15 miles south of Lorain, is Oberlin College, a pioneer in breaking down educational discrimination against women and blacks. It was among the first institutions in the country to award degrees to both. The campus is situated around Tappan Square in the heart of town. The Allen Memorial Art Museum is open during the academic year on Tuesday, 1:00 to 8:00; Wednesday through Friday, 11:00 to 5:00; weekends, 2:00 to 5:00. At other times of the year it is open Wednesday to Sunday, 2:00 to 5:00. There is no admission charge.

State Parks on the Lake

Geneva—on Ohio 534 north of Geneva, has swimming, fishing, and day-use facilities.

Headlands Beach—northwest of Painesville on Ohio 44, has swimming, fishing, and day-use facilities.

If you go: Spend the entire time in Cleveland.

1. Take the downtown walk outlined in this chapter.

2. Visit the museums in the University Circle area.

3. Drive east to the Garfield Home in Mentor, the Kirtland Temple, and the nautical museum in Fairport.

4. Take the scenic lakeshore drive west to the Lake Erie Nature Center. Visit the Oberlin campus and Allen Memorial Art Museum.

5. Take a side trip to the Hale Farm in the Cuyahoga Valley National Recreation Area. Continue to Akron to see Stan Hywet Hall.

6. Explore Ohio City, take a Cuyahoga River cruise, visit the Metro Zoo.

7. Drive east to see Shandy Hall, Ashtabula's Bridge Street area, and the Railroad Museum in Conneaut.

The most decisive naval battle in Great Lakes history was fought within sight of the Perry Victory Memorial, Put-in-Bay.

7

Sandusky Bay to Toledo

Erie is a hard-working lake. Like a plodding drudge it tends to business, while its more glamorous sisters go gadding about. Its most characteristic ship is the giant freighter rather than the dancing sailboat. Its cities are shirtsleeve towns, while factories and coal docks cluster about its shores.

But even a lake like Erie needs a respite from labor, a holiday corner where business is forgotten for a little dash of gaiety. Its southernmost extremity is Erie's place for pleasure. Islands dot its surface here. Roller coasters run merrily amok amid the screams of young riders. Instead of factories there are wineries here and quiet towns dispense the pleasures of a pre-industrial age. The area is known generally as Lake Erie Vacationland and it centers around the pleasant old town of Sandusky. Erie's Vacationland extends from Vermilion on the east to Port Clinton on the west, a distance of about 35 miles if you drive right through. No one would want to do a thing like that, though. One of the most intensive concentrations of tourist attractions on the Lakes is contained in this small area. Much of it is hokey, but it is all in fun. For an industrious lake, Erie knows how to have a good time.

Improbably enough, this playground was once a battle-ground. The area around Sandusky Bay was claimed by both French and British and each colonial government took turns destroying the forts of the other. Pontiac wiped out the garrison in 1763 after it had passed to British control. Mad Anthony Wayne finally broke the Indian power at Fallen Timbers, just west of Toledo, in a battle that opened the Northwest to settlement. Desperate engagements were fought at Fort Meigs at Perrysburg and Fort Stephenson at Fremont against invading British and Indians in the War of 1812. Finally, Commodore Perry ended British ambitions in the West for good with his crushing victory off Put-in-Bay in 1813. In the waters where the American and British fleets grappled to the death, weekend boaters now swarm; and Fallen Timbers is almost lost among Toledo's expanding suburbs. The blessings of peace.

The land as far as the western shore of Sandusky Bay was part of the Connecticut tract which the state reserved for its own residents after the Revolutionary War. This portion was called the Firelands, because it was intended specifically for those who had been burned out during the war. Many of the towns have a strong New England sense to them; places like Milan look as if they had been dropped down intact from somewhere south of Hartford.

Huron was settled in 1805. Vermilion three years later. The site of the old fort on the bay grew into the settlement of Ogontz, later changed to the more manageable Sandusky. The rich quarries on the Marblehead Peninsula brought settlers into that area around 1821. A group of westbound immigrants was shipwrecked at the mouth of the Portage River and decided to stay right where they were. That is how Port Clinton began in 1827. In the next decade, permanent settlers took up residence on South Bass and Kelleys islands.

For a time, that is where the westward movement stalled. The lakeshore west to the mouth of the Maumee River was swamp, part of the Black Swamp, extending far inland and presenting a formidable barrier to expansion. There were settle-ments a few miles up the river at Perrysburg and Maumee, but deep-draft ships could not make it that far up the Maumee

River. So Toledo was founded as a port at the edge of the swamp in 1836, and allegedly named after the city in Spain by Washington Irving who had a brother living here.

Like so many cities on the Lake Erie shore, Toledo's growth really began with the completion of a canal. When the Wabash and Erie Canal opened in 1845 the city's population tripled in a twinkling. With Toledo growing, the impetus for draining the Black Swamp was irresistible. The job was undertaken by recently arrived German immigrants in 1850 and the settlement of Ohio's Erie coast moved on to completion. Even today, however, the area between Port Clinton and Toledo is a marshy, sparsely populated region, where hunters and fishermen are more at home than farmers.

While the Sandusky Bay area turned to commercial fishing, tourism, and wine production, Toledo was a city in search of an industry. The hunt ended in 1888 when Edward D. Libbey moved his company here from New England. Henceforth, Toledo's special product would be glass. It was not quite that straightforward, though. Many of Libbey's workmen quit to return home and the quality of his product waned. Fortunately, he had the foresight to hire a genius, Michael Owens, as a foreman. In 1901 Owens developed the automatic glass bottle maker, revolutionizing the industry. It not only speeded production but also dramatically improved levels of hygiene.

Owens founded the Owens Bottle Machine Company, which in turn became Owens-Illinois. He then turned his attention to sheet glass, and with Libbey and another Toledo glassmaker, Edward Ford, organized Libbey-Owens-Ford in 1930. Also headquartered in Toledo and engaged primarily in fiberglass manufacture are Owens-Corning and Johns-Manville. The glass they produce, fortunately, is a good deal clearer than the interconnected company structures.

Put-in-Bay

Its real name is South Bass Island but no one but a mapmaker would call it anything but Put-in-Bay. There are, unarguably, a North Bass and a Middle Bass island nearby. But for generations boaters have sought the natural harbor here as a place to put-in, and the harbor's function was gradually extended to name the entire island.

The place has been a holiday island for well over a century, just about as long as its wineries have been turning out Catawba wines. The first record of a resort in this area of Lake Erie was at Ruggles Beach on the mainland in 1856. Within three years, though, Put-in-Bay was famous for its convivial July Fourth celebrations. Its hotels, especially the sprawling Victory, were noted for their wealthy clientele. By the 1870s it was one of the most fashionable spas in the country.

This condition did not last long. Excursion steamers from Cleveland, Toledo, and Detroit began carrying passengers for day-trip cruises to the island, scandalizing most affluent vacationers who packed up for more exclusive precincts. The carryings-on, even on the Sabbath, profoundly disturbed financier Jay Cooke who owned Gibraltar Island in the middle of the harbor. He protested vainly about the raucous Sunday celebrants. By 1919 the last vestige of the old carriage trade disappeared when the Victory Hotel burned to the ground. Then after the Depression, when an automobile ride began holding more appeal than a leisurely day on a lake cruiser, the excursion trade dried up. Today the emphasis is on pleasure boaters who come in on their own craft, day-trippers who make the twenty-minute ferryboat ride from Catawba on the mainland, and seekers after nostalgic settings.

It is a pleasantly outdated sort of place. Its quiet lanes and country roads are perfect for bicycling and rentals are available a five-minute walk up from the ferry dock. A tour train also makes circuits of the island, starting from this area. The main street of town wears the previous century well. The Colonial, a dance hall and refreshment pavilion built in 1907, was the last of the grand resort facilities to be built on the island. It is still in operation as a "family recreation center," just down the block from the circular red form of the Round House Bar, reassembled on this spot in 1873 from its original resting place in Toledo. ("You can't get cornered around here," is its boast.) Other buildings of that time make up the rest of the business district. They all face a waterfront park, a five-acre tract given to the public in 1866 by Rivera de San Jargo who then owned the entire island. The park, displaying cannon and shot from Perry's victory on the lake, overlooks the harbor and a marina.

At the far end of the island, on the western shore, about one mile distant, there is a state park and public dock. It is the perfect place for sitting and watching the lake slap in after a picnic at the adjacent grove. For best results, the picnic should be accompanied by a bottle of some of the local wine. This can be picked up en route to the park at the Heineman tasting room, last of the local wineries open to the public. Cultivation of grapes was begun here predominantly by German immigrants from the Rhineland and the older wineries still bear the names of the founders.

Near the winery is the Perry Cave, another big attraction on the island. The commodore reputedly stored ammunition here for some reason best known to him. The cave later stored British prisoners. Another of the island caves, Crystal Cave, is right on the Heineman grounds. Both are open from Memorial Day to Labor Day.

If you come from the Catawba boat dock to town, you will pass right by the island airport. During the winter months when the lake ices over, this is the only contact with the mainland.

Most visitors, though, will want to take a look at the Perry Victory Monument. At 352 feet in height it is a very big deal indeed. Sentiment for constructing a local memorial of some kind to the 1813 Battle of Lake Erie grew stronger as the nineteenth century waned, fueled perhaps by the fervent Independence Day celebrations here. Jay Cooke wanted it on his own Gibraltar Island. But as the centennial of the battle neared, the focus shifted to Put-in-Bay. The manager of the Victory Hotel is credited with building public enthusiasm for the project. By 1908 the state of Ohio agreed to help with the financing.

Three years later, the federal government and eight other states agreed to pitch in, too. The Army Corps of Engineers picked the site on the island's eastern end, adjacent to the town. The design selected by a special committee is a Doric fluted column, forty-five feet in diameter at the base, topped by an observation platform and twenty-three-foot high urn. The cornerstone was laid on July 4, 1913. The remains of six officers killed in the engagement—three American and three British—were transferred to the base in September. In 1915 the monument opened to the public and has been a crowd-pleaser ever since. In 1972 its name was officially changed to Perry's Victory and International Peace Memorial since it also commemorates the peaceful frontier between Canada and the United States created in the aftermath of the War of 1812.

The view from the top is worth the elevator ride up. The Ohio mainland, town and island, the marina, the Cooke mansion (now owned by Ohio State University), and other islands dotting the water spread out in an unforgettable panorama. On a clear day you can easily see Pelee Island, which is Canadian territory. It may seem odd to be standing in Ohio and looking at Canada; but the lake narrows significantly at this point and Pelee is the southernmost part of Canada—farther south, in fact, than some parts of California. The monument is open daily, early April to mid-October. There is a charge for the elevator ride.

The battle actually took place closer to North Bass Island, 10 miles north by northwest of this point. Put-in-Bay was Perry's headquarters. He came here from Presque Isle, Pennsylvania, following the construction of half his fleet in the Erie shipyards. The British commodore, Barclay, retreated up the Detroit River upon learning that Perry was on the lake. For a month the Americans waited for the British to emerge from the river to fight. On September 9, 1813, Barclay obliged them. The Americans had the advantage in firepower and ships; the British had an edge in battle experience. Each side carried about 440 men into battle.

Perry's flagship, the *Lawrence,* was matched against the *Detroit,* largest of the British vessels. The battle began shortly after noon on September 10. Perry's ship took a fearful battering from the *Detroit*. His other brig, the *Niagara*, stayed completely out of the fight, though. After three hours, the *Lawrence* was helpless and four-fifths of its crew were dead or wounded. Undaunted, Perry crossed to the undamaged *Niagara* in an open rowboat with a handful of men and renewed the battle. He made right for the two British brigs, loosing a withering fire on them. The two ships collided trying to escape. Within fifteen minutes after he boarded the *Niagara*, Perry had his victory. "We have met the enemy and they are ours," he wrote to General Harrison who waited anxiously on shore with his army. "Two ships, two brigs, one schooner & one sloop." The Americans had wrested control of the western lakes from Britain. In this sector of the war, at least, Britain had been beaten decisively; and the West made secure for expansion.

Vermilion

For a few years in the middle of the last century, Vermilion entertained ambitions of rivalling Cleveland as a lake metropolis. It had one of the best harbors on Lake Erie. Vermilion lake captains were regarded as the most skillful in the business. Captain Alva Bradley opened his shipyards here in 1841 and they brought immediate prosperity to the town on the banks of the Vermilion River (so called for the red dye that Indians made from the mud in its banks.) But the larger city just had too much going for it and Vermilion could not compete. The final blow came in 1859 when Captain Bradley moved his operations to Cleveland.

If it was really a blow, though, it was far from crushing. Vermilion, instead of steaming full tilt into the industrial age, dropped out of the current. For about a century it remained just beyond the orbit of metropolitan Cleveland and a little outside the burgeoning resorts of Sandusky Bay. Travelers passed through without ever knowing or caring what had once been in this little town.

In 1953, the Great Lakes Historical Society, then based in the Cleveland Public Library, moved into new quarters, a lakeside mansion left to the society in trust by the Wakefield family of Vermilion. It began publishing a quarterly journal and developed its museum into what is probably the best of its kind on the Lakes. By 1968 there was enough interest to add a modern $250,000 wing to the old house. Vermilion had become something of a tourist stop. Many visitors walked out of the museum and lingered, delighted by the shady streets and old homes built by lake mariners, a century before. At one time, forty-two lake captains made Vermilion their home port. Their homes were built on the side streets of town and they have come down the years in fine fashion.

Vermilion, sensing it might have something here, set about to dress up its main thoroughfare, Liberty Avenue, which carries traffic on the lakeshore route between Cleveland and Sandusky. The old houses were researched and catalogued. Soon a French restaurant opened—a certain harbinger of fine

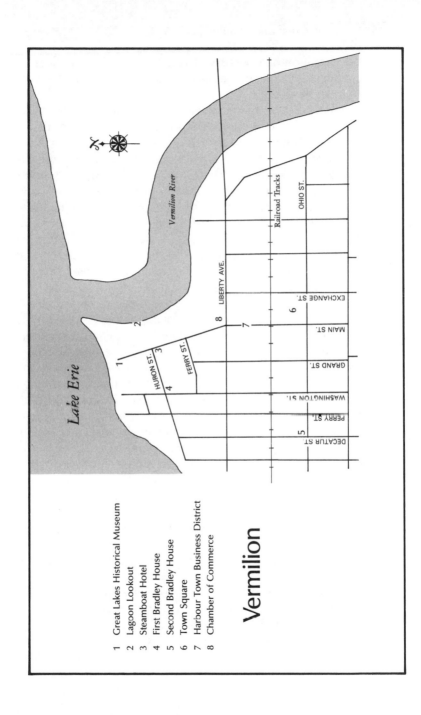

Vermilion

1 Great Lakes Historical Museum
2 Lagoon Lookout
3 Steamboat Hotel
4 First Bradley House
5 Second Bradley House
6 Town Square
7 Harbour Town Business District
8 Chamber of Commerce

Lake Erie

Vermilion River

Railroad Tracks

LIBERTY AVE.

OHIO ST.
EXCHANGE ST.
MAIN ST.
GRAND ST.
WASHINGTON ST.
FERRY ST.
DECATUR ST.

HURON ST.
FERRY ST.

things. Vermilion had become Harbour Town 1837, an attempt to recreate the look and ambience of the place in the year it was incorporated.

It is now one of the most delightful old towns on the lakes, a treat for nostalgic strollers. The Great Lakes Museum at the foot of Main Street is the best place to start. Its new wing, built on the lines of a ship, houses a treasure trove of artifacts relating to the Lakes and the men who sailed them. A ship's bridge has been reconstructed, looking out over the lake, complete with navigation instruments and engine-room console. There are models of famous ships, paintings of the Lake, antique instruments, and a room dedicated to the history of Vermilion. Open daily in summer, 11:00 to 6:00; spring and fall, 11:00 to 5:00; winter, 11:00 to 5:00, weekends only. There is an admission charge.

From the museum, walk south one block to Huron Street, then turn east to the park overlooking the lagoons on the opposite bank of the river. This development is an enchanting sight, with each frame house backing on a waterway like a Midwestern Venice. The cruisers enter the harbor, turn into the lagoons, and tie up right at the owner's back door.

Across the street is the rambling old Steamboat Hotel, portions of which date to 1838. Huron Street contains many homes built in the 1840s during the city's greatest years of prosperity. Alva Bradley constructed his home at 5679 Huron Street in 1840. Bradley's second home is on the corner of Ohio and Decatur streets. Most of the old houses have a strong New England sense to them, a saltbox kind of architecture rather than the more rambling model that is more usual in the Midwest. That and the rocky shoreline give Vermilion a definite eastern character.

There are other concentrations of old homes along Washington Street, south to Ohio Street and then eastward. Ohio Street, across the railroad tracks from the business district, developed a bit later than many of its homes are Victorian in style, dating from the 1880s.

At Ohio and Main streets is the square, with the town hall and opera house holding down one corner. The railroad tracks at the north end spoil the effect of the square somewhat, though. Liberty Avenue and Main Street contain most of the town's business establishments, all decked out in 1830s style. Among them is a very nice Czech restaurant which complements the French operation on the waterfront.

Excellent walking maps of Vermilion can be picked up at the Chamber of Commerce office, on Liberty Avenue just east of Main Street.

Cedar Point

Please do not call Cedar Point a theme park. That is the newest catchphrase in the amusement park business, one of the fastest growing branches of the travel industry. It was originated by the Walt Disney organization when it opened Southern California's Disneyland in the mid-1950s. Cedar Point is simply an amusement park. No highfalutin themes here. Just good old fun.

It was the rebirth that Disney gave the business, however, that saved venerable Cedar Point from the wrecking ball. There has been an amusement park on this sandy Lake Erie spit on the eastern edge of Sandusky since 1870. But by 1956, just as Disneyland was opening, Cedar Point was getting ready to close for good. New owners were developing plans to turn it into a residential complex. Crowds had diminished and the place was in a sad state of repair. Its grand old hotel, the Breakers, was a rotting hulk. Its rides were outmoded, its midway a shambles.

Cedar Point, like most of the country's amusement parks, had reached a peak of success in the years preceding World War I. But changing tastes and rising affluence seemingly had made them anachronisms. To the new generation an exciting evening out meant a movie, not a ride on the Ferris wheel. The accelerating pace of life turned rides that were thrilling to a previous age into the humdrum. But Disney showed what could be done with the old amusement park concept using imagination, a family orientation, and lots of money. With the incredible success of Disneyland, and later Walt Disney World in Florida, imitators sprung up in every corner of the country. They tried for similar techniques. Central to the operation was the idea of the theme park. Supposedly the attractions in each section of the park would be unified by a common theme—be it geographic, historic, ethnic, or whatever. The geographic themes were sometimes wobbly and the historical themes were of the comic strip variety. The elements of the parks were often interchangeable mass-produced components. But none of that was important. All that mattered was the theme.

The new owners of Cedar Point saw what was afoot. The

residential plans were scrapped and by 1959 a new Cedar Point began to take shape. It would use the family orientation and the imagination that Disney had pioneered. But instead of copying the formats of the theme parks, the park would remain rooted in its own place and history. Cedar Point grew originally because it was situated on Lake Erie. So one of the first elements of the new park was a marina to serve the lake trade. There would be a tentative nod at a theme with Frontier Town, but there would also be a Frontier Trail in which solid local history would be interwoven. The Breakers was restored to the grandeur of its 1904 opening, but with rates a bit higher than that 1904 season's $10 a week. The Coliseum, which had opened two years later, was also spruced up. The midway was adorned with floral arrangements that gave the old walk a certain raffish charm. The food service was upgraded. About $16 million was poured into the park. And gradually the crowds began to return.

On a summer weekend in the 1980s it is hard to believe this place ever was in danger of going out of business. The cars flock across the causeway from the mainland and park 25 and 30 deep in the lots. Crowds swarm through the gates into the midway. On peak weekends the waits easily can reach an hour at the most popular rides. It is common for high schools from more than 150 miles away to plan senior trips around a weekend in the park. Reservations at nearby motels must be made weeks in advance during the season. The park is open from mid-May to Labor Day; weekends only in September. A single admission price covers all rides.

"We do not try to build a plastic universe of the perfect here," says a park spokesman. "All we are is an amusement park." But the park does go along with the trends. When wild animals started getting big, Cedar Point added Jungle Larry's African Sarfari. When giant movies came in, the Point installed a gigantic IMAX screen, enveloping the viewer within a seven-story high wall of sight and sound. When the new, twisting roller coaster rides were developed, it added the Corkscrew and did turn-away business for turned-around stomachs. (There are six roller coasters and fifty-seven rides in all on the grounds.)

And for those who go looking, there are a few markers of note on the premises, too. One of them points out that in 1910 aviator Glenn Curtiss flew 64 miles from the beach here to Cleveland—the longest trip over water in an airplane at that time. The other marker relates that on the same beach a few summers later Notre Dame football players Gus Dorais and Knute Rockne developed the forward pass while working as lifeguards here, thereby changing the face of an entire sport.

It is a place not without a history.

Other Things to See

[1] Just west of Ruggles Beach on U.S. 6, where Old Woman Creek flows into Lake Erie near a driftwood-strewn beach, is the southernmost point of the Great Lakes, approximately 41 , 23 .'

[2] The great inventor Thomas Edison was born in Milan, Ohio, in a frame house backing on the canal that had once made the village a lively grain shipping port. Edison's home, in which he lived until the age of seven, is open April through November, Tuesday through Saturday, from 9:00 to 5:00; Sunday, from 1:00 to 5:00; February and March, weekends only; rest of year by appointment. Across the street, at 10 Edison Drive, a historical museum displays the town's surprisingly colorful past. Open January through November; 9:00 to 5:00 in summer, 1:00 to 5:00 in spring and fall; Sunday, 1:00 to 5:00. Closed Monday. On the lovely Public Square, the Milan Inn has been dispensing cheer and warmth since 1845.

[3] Daily trips across Lake Erie leave from Sandusky aboard the M.V. *Pelee Islander* during the summer months. The boat returns from either Kingsville or Leamington, Ontario, with a stop at Canada's Pelee Island. The boat carries cars but you can also make the trip just as a passenger. Call locally for rates and schedules. The dock is at the foot of Jackson Street.

[4] Up from unknown depths come the waters of the Blue Hole in Castalia. The artesian spring water then flows off into trout streams. It is on Ohio 269, south from Ohio 2. Open Memorial Day through Labor Day, 9:00 to 8:00; closed, mid-October to mid-April; rest of year, weekends only, 10:00 to 5:00. There is an admission charge. Picnic area.

[5] Kelleys Island is the largest on the American side of the lake. There are 2,800 acres and a state park there. Grooves left by the glaciers of the last Ice Age, as they scrunched across the land, can be seen on the island's north coast, one of the more dramatic evidences of that epoch. Inscription Rock, bearing pictographs carved by the Eriez Indians in the seventeenth century, is protected by a canopy on the southern coast. There are also abandoned limestone quarries and interesting old buildings on this peaceful island. There is frequent ferry service from

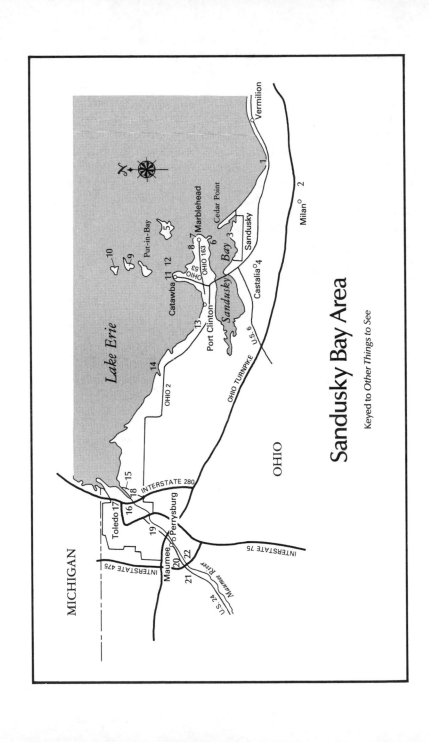

Sandusky Bay Area

Keyed to Other Things to See

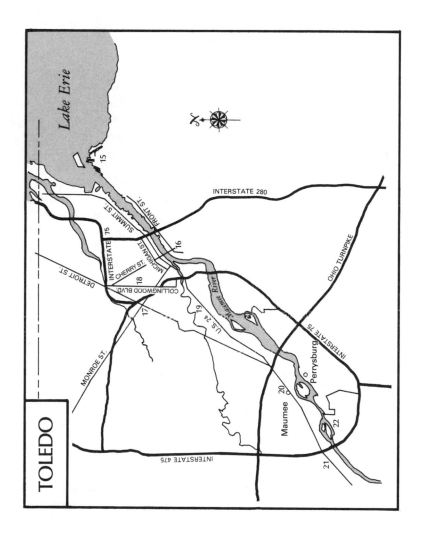

Marblehead on the Neuman Boat Line, Inc., with limited summer departures from Sandusky, as well. Island Airlines also flies in.

[6]   Johnson's Island, off the southern end of Marblehead Peninsula, was used as a Confederate prison camp and it holds a cemetery in which 206 southern soldiers are buried. A causeway connects it to the mainland, but visitors are not encouraged.

[7]   The Marblehead Light, just east of the town of Marblehead, is the oldest in continuous service on the lake. It was built in 1821–22 on a rocky promontory and is a favorite spot for fishermen and gazers and idlers. The spot commands a fine view of the lively boat traffic and of Kelleys Island across the water.

[8]   Lakeside is something like the Midwest's answer to Chautauqua, with a summer program of concerts, plays, and lectures. It is operated by the United Methodist Church and has run every summer since 1873. West of Marblehead, off Ohio 163.

[9]   Middle Bass Island offers winery tours at the Lonz operation. There are mainly vines and seclusion here. The island is accessible from Port Clinton by Island Airlines and Parker Boat Lines.

[10]   North Bass, or Isle of St. George, has even more vines and even greater seclusion. There are no tourist facilities and day visitors are asked to register with the superintendent. Meier's Wine Cellars owns most of the island. Accessible from Port Clinton by Island Airlines.

[11]   Put-in-Bay is just a twenty-minute cruise on the Miller Boat Line from Catawba, on the northern tip of the Marblehead Peninsula on Ohio 53. There are twelve daily scheduled departures during the summer, more on the weekends. Call for schedule and rates.

[12]   Mouse Island, just off the dock at Catawba, was once a presidential retreat. It was owned by the family of Rutherford B. Hayes who came from nearby Fremont.

[13]   There are swimming and picnic grounds in Port Clinton's Lakeview Park. The Parker Boat Line, Inc., operates

scheduled service to Put-in-Bay with seven boats daily in summer. Service to Middle Bass by appointment. The landing is downtown, just off Ohio 163. Island Airlines has its main offices at the airstrip just east of town on Ohio 163. Check locally for rates and schedules.

[14] The last nesting grounds of the bald eagle on the Great Lakes is found in the Ottawa National Wildlife Refuge. The facility on Lake Erie, with the adjacent Crane Creek State Park, is mostly sedge marsh and is one of the top wildfowl observatories in the Midwest.

[15] The Port of Toledo is one of the busiest on the lakes, with coal and iron ore its top cargoes. A viewing platform enables you to watch the activity near the overseas cargo center. Exit from Interstate 280 at Front Street, head east and follow the signs.

[16] There are two ways of exploring the Toledo riverfront and both methods depart from the area of the Cherry Street Bridge, on the east side of the river. Cruises aboard the *Arawanna II* operate from Memorial Day to Labor Day, on weekend afternoons, from 1:15 to 4:15. They depart from International Park. If you prefer to remain land based, the Waterfront Electric Railway covers much of the same territory aboard a former Chicago El car. Its operating times are the same as the cruises and it also runs through the park.

[17] Where else but Toledo would you expect to find the world's finest collection of glass artwork? Glass magnate Edward Libbey founded the Toledo Museum of Art, after all. It is an engrossing assortment of pieces, ranging from ancient Syria to Renaissance Venice to the most modern concepts, all beautifully displayed. There is much more in one of the country's great art museums. It is on Monroe at Scottwood Street, 1 mile west of downtown. Open Tuesday through Saturday, from 9:00 to 5:00; Sunday 1:00 to 5:00; free.

[18] The Old West End of Toledo has one of the most concentrated collections of Victorian architecture in the Midwest, as a walk along Collingwood Boulevard will quickly reveal. Along the way, you will also pass the cathedral of the Toledo

Diocese, a splendid Spanish Gothic structure clearly inspired by that of its namesake city in Castile.

[19]   The Toledo Zoo calls itself "America's Most Complete Zoo" and it has a good case for the claim. Besides its 2,258 representatives of 557 species there is also a horticultural center, museum of health and natural history, aquarium, theater, and children's zoo. It is on U.S. 24, southwest of downtown Toledo. Open all year, admission charge; parking fee from April to September.

[20]   James Wolcott arrived in Ohio from Connecticut in 1827, bought land west of Maumee, and opened a steamboat-landing on the river. He married the granddaughter of Little Turtle and eventually became a judge and mayor of Maumee. His dignified home, occupied by his descendants until 1957, is now a pioneer museum of the area, operated by the Maumee Valley Historical Society. Other historic Maumee Valley structures, including a railroad depot and log cabin, have been moved to the site, as well. Open Tuesday to Sunday, April to December, 1:00 to 4:00; admission charge. It is located on the River Road.

[21]   One of the turning points in American history came at Fallen Timbers when Anthony Wayne's army routed the Indian forces of Little Turtle and opened the rich land of northern Ohio and the Northwest beyond to settlement. The place was given its odd name because a tornado had mowed down trees in the vicinity just a few days before the battle in 1794. A monument marks the spot on a ridge overlooking the Maumee River on U.S. 24, just west of Interstate 475, a few miles west of the town of Maumee.

[22]   A few years later, though, the area was the focus of combat again. A British force out of Detroit attacked the army of General William Henry Harrison at Fort Meigs, which had been built to guard against just such an assault. For twelve days in the spring of 1813 the British laid siege to the fort, just west of Perrysburg. Eventually they had to retire, though, and Harrison's forces came out of the affair intact. The fort, restored as a bicentennial project, is open Memorial Day to Labor Day,

Wednesday through Saturday, 9:30 to 5:00; Sundays, noon to 5:00; admission charge.

Side Trips

The Bluebird Special steam railroad makes scenic weekend trips along the Maumee River from Grand Rapids, Ohio, to Waterville, Ohio. It leaves on its sixty-minute jaunt on weekends and holidays at noon and 3:00, Memorial Day through October. The depot, at Third and Mill streets, Grand Rapids, is 24 miles southwest of Toledo on U.S. 24 and Ohio 578.

The Rutherford B. Hayes Home and Museum, Spiegel Grove, is located in Fremont, 28 miles southwest of Sandusky. Also in town are relics of the odd battle of Fort Stephenson in which a handful of men armed with a single aging cannon held off an attacking force of British and Indians in 1813. The site is now the Birchard Library downtown and there is a museum in the basement.

Clyde is only an alias. This Ohio town was actually the model for Sherwood Anderson's classic of twentieth-century fiction, *Winesburg, Ohio*. A devotee of the book will still be able to pick out landmarks mentioned in its pages. A new restaurant, the Winesburg Inn, formally acknowledges the town's connection to Anderson's rather judgemental book, a tie that was ignored by the scandalized townsfolk for a good fifty years. Clyde is located just east of Fremont on U.S. 20.

South of Bellevue are the Seneca Caverns which were created by earthquake action. They are about 27 miles south-southwest of Sandusky.

The Firelands Museum in Norwalk shows relics of pioneer days in this section of the Western Reserve. The town is 17 miles south of Sandusky.

State Parks on the Lake

Crane Creek—24 miles east of Toledo, off Ohio 2, has swimming, fishing, and picnic facilities. No camping.

Catawba—17 miles north-northwest of Sandusky, off Ohio 53, has fishing and picnic grounds. No swimming or camping.

East Harbor—15 miles north-northwest of Sandusky, off Ohio 269, has complete water facilities, swimming, a nature program, and 570 campsites.

South Bass—on the western end of the island, has fishing and boating. No beach but swimming is permitted. Cabins available and 150 campsites.

Kelleys Island—on the north shore of the island, has fishing, boating, picnic grounds, and swimming, along with 150 campsites.

If you go for a weekend: Stay in Sandusky.

1. Drive to Vermilion to see the Great Lakes Museum and the old homes. Stay for dinner at one of the town's restaurants.

2. Spend the day at Cedar Point.

3. Drive to Catawba and catch the ferry to South Bass Island. Rent a bike and explore the island.

Cedar Point Amusement Park has dispensed good times for more than a century on Ohio's Lake Erie Shore.

If you go for a week: Stay in Sandusky for four nights and in Toledo for three nights.

1–3. Same as the weekend tour.

4. Drive around the Marblehead Peninsula. Take a ferry to Kelleys Island.

5. Visit the Blue Hole and the Rutherford B. Hayes Home and Museum in Fremont. Continue on to Toledo.

6. Spend the day at the Art Museum and explore the adjacent Collingwood Boulevard area.

7. Visit Fort Meigs, Fallen Timbers, the Wolcott House, and the port area.

The glistening towers of the riverside Renaissance Center symbolize the hopes for the city of Detroit's rebirth.

Detroit and Its River

The night shift engineer for the Detroit Edison Company was perplexed. In his enthusiasm to build a machine he called a quadricycle in the shed behind his home, he had neglected one thing, an exit door to get the fool thing out onto the street. He had his doubts that this motorcar would even work, but he went this far so he decided he might as well see it all the way through. He tore down part of the shed wall, rolled his contraption out to Bagley Street, and went to start it up. And much to Henry Ford's surprise, as he told his wife later that night, "the darned thing ran."

It was June, 1896, five years short of Detroit's 200th birthday. It was an old city by Midwestern standards, founded as a fort by the French before anyone had settled New Orleans or St. Louis. There were still many families in the area who traced their histories back to the first French farmers of the early eighteenth century. But the most influential men in town were the lumber barons. They had made their fortunes in the pine forests of northern Michigan and lined the main arteries of Detroit with their mansions. They had made it into a gracious city, regarded by many visitors as among the loveliest in the country. Not terribly important in the national economic picture, Detroit seemingly was quite content to leave things at that. By the turn of the century it had a population of 280,000—about the same size as Milwaukee at that time.

The city had some small industries. It was a center for marine gasoline engines and coach bodies, as well as a hub of transportation for the Great Lakes. But the timber industry was nearly depleted. A great labor pool was forming in the lumber camps of the North and the city's richest men were seeking new outlets for their vast accumulations of capital.

All these factors fused on that June night in 1896. It was Detroit's destiny that Henry Ford pushed through his shed wall. Within twenty years the city would be transformed utterly. The leisurely old river town would become the center of American industry, a booming metropolis of one million people. Its past, its rich history would be virtually annihilated by the feverish rush of events. By the 1920s, Detroit would be as rootless and mobile as the new Americans that its chief product was creating. It had become a city molded by its own invention. The automobile had reshaped Detroit in its own image. There have been many adjectives used to describe the city in recent years. Gracious, however, has never been one of them.

It began as a strategic link in the French colonial empire. The most cursory glance at a map will show you why. The Strait of Detroit (the city's name actually means "Strait" in French) controls access between the upper and lower Great Lakes. Whoever controlled it would be in command of all trade, all communication between Mackinac and the newly discovered southern route across Lakes Ontario and Erie. Sieur de la Mothe Cadillac was sent from Montreal to fortify the place. But the French also wanted this to be a permanent outpost, unlike their other western forts which existed merely to serve the fur trade. Detroit would have farmers, civilian residents to maintain it as a bulwark against the expanding English to the south. Cadillac approached from the traditional French route, down from Georgian Bay to the north. He landed on July 24, 1701, and within hours had begun the construction of Fort Ponchartrain du Detroit.

The city was still a tiny farming village when the British

took it over in 1760 as a prize of the French and Indian War. The garrison narrowly escaped massacre when the local Indians under Pontiac rose in rebellion against their new overlords. As it was, nearby settlers, a relief column, and a small expeditionary force were wiped out before the five-month siege was lifted.

The Revolution was a distant rumor in Detroit, although the British used the fort as a base for raids on isolated western settlements. Its lieutenant-governor Henry Hamilton was cursed on the frontier as the "hair-buyer of Detroit." It took Anthony Wayne's victory at Fallen Timbers to finally dislodge the British from the outpost in 1796. Nine years later the place burned to the ground. That calamity, however, cleared the way for Detroit to break away from the limits of the old French settlement and begin expanding. Judge Augustus B. Woodward was in charge of rebuilding the city and developed the plan that has confounded visitors ever since. Enamored of Charles L'Enfant's design for Washington, D.C., he sought to build Detroit in a fan-shaped arrangement, with avenues radiating out from central squares. That worked for a while but soon the city decided to go ahead with a straightaway grid plan and superimposed it on Woodward's design. The result is sheer chaos, at least in the downtown area.

With the completion of the Erie Canal, Detroit's growth began. It was the transshipment point between the East and the newly opened farmlands of fertile southern Michigan. Later in the century the wealth of the north country poured into the city. At this point Ford and his friends entered the picture.

Detroit today is an unsettling mixture of deep despair and incredible promise. In recent years it has been shaken by the country's greatest middle-class departure to the suburbs, its bloodiest race riots, its highest crime rate. Its name is virtually synonymous with the collapse of the urban dream in America.

It is not, however, a totally unlovely place. It is a city of trees and residential blocks. An enormous ratio of single-family homes has been its hallmark for years. Viewed from a height it looks like a garden town, with mile after mile of tree-lined neighborhoods stretching off to the horizon on the Michigan plain. Seen from across the river it presents one of the country's most powerful skylines. By night it is a spectacle of magic, especially in summer when the lake freighters roll past on the Detroit River. Its Belle Isle is a unique facility, an island park in the Detroit River in the midst of the city. Many residential areas of the city—Indian Village on the east side, Palmer Woods on the west—are revelations to visitors who expected only grime and pollution. Some of its suburbs, the Grosse Pointes and Bloomfield Hills, are among the wealthiest in America.

Now the city has turned back to the river again. Renaissance Center, the largest privately financed development in the country's history, opened in 1977. It rises on the riverfront, a few hundred yards east of the place at which Cadillac landed, and its prime mover, Henry Ford II, is the grandson of the man who remade the city economically with his motorcar.

Greenfield Village and the Henry Ford Museum

There is a photograph in Greenfield Village, in the Wright Brothers Cycle Shop, that symbolizes the intent of Henry Ford's museums better than anything else. It was taken in about 1910 and shows one of the Wrights in a pioneer aircraft soaring over a carriage occupied by one of Europe's monarchs. The coachmen are gripping the reins of the terrified horses and a viewer can sense the utter astonishment of the carriage's occupants at the sight of a machine flying over them. They are royal but cannot fly. Do they sense that the forces represented by this flying machine are about to sweep away the comfortable, secure, privileged world they know? Can they hear the distant drumming?

It is this moment in time—the instant of tension between the agricultural world that Ford knew as a boy and the mechanized world that he helped to create—that he tried to preserve in this museum complex. It is as much a tribute to the inventive genius and the mechanical skills of Ford's contemporaries as it is a monument to the world that genius destroyed.

The complex includes two separate museums. They are generally linked under one description because they are adjacent. But they require two separate admissions and contain too much to even skim their surfaces in a single day. If you are pressed for time, spend it in Greenfield Village and save the Henry Ford Museum for later. The museum is a fine facility, with its exhibits on the mechanical arts and furnishings and its street of early American Shops. But the village is unique, a haunting evocation of a vanished America.

The complex is formally known as the Edison Institute, named for a man whom Ford admired above all others. Young Ford worked in the Detroit Edison Company and was encouraged by the great inventor to persevere in his efforts to build a motorcar. In 1929, thirty-three years after Ford's initial success, he brought the old man and President Hoover to Dearborn to formally open the village. It was named after the farm settlement on nearby Greenfield Road in which Ford had been born in 1863. Three days after the opening came the crash of the stock market and the unleashing of irresistible social forces that would destroy the final remnants of that village life.

The village is divided into several sections. There is the business district along Main Street near the entrance. An industrial section lies to the left, while on the right is the residential area. At the far end of the village is Suwanee Park, a small amusement area. Near the center of it is the Village Green, with inn, church, and assembly hall. Finally, there are the reconstructed laboratories of Edison's workshop in Menlo Park, New Jersey, where he labored on many of his inventions. This was one of the most significant parts of the village in Ford's mind. The Menlo Park setting is absolutely accurate, right down to the soil in the compound which Ford had imported from New Jersey.

The village is an eclectic sort of place, with structures brought here from all over the country—many of them escaping demolition because of the move. There is the cycle shop of the Wrights from Dayton, Ohio; the courthouse which once heard Lincoln's legal arguments from Logan County, Illinois; Noah Webster's home from New Haven, Connecticut. There is even a jewelry shop from London and a collection of farm buildings and cottages from the Cotswold Hills of England. But the overall look is second generation New England, the sort of village built in nineteenth-century Michigan by its settlers from the Northeast.

It is an ideal community. Stephen Foster writes his songs right across the street from Luther Burbank, hard at work on his plants. Stern Mr. McGuffey runs the schoolhouse and young Abe Lincoln is practicing law over at the court. Edison is busy perfecting the electric light in his lab while the brothers Wright are tinkering with an even stranger device in their shop. And a forever young Henry Ford is on the job at the Edison Illuminating Company, looking just as he did in 1893 when he was made chief engineer. The original plant is gone from its location on Washington Boulevard and State Street in downtown Detroit. But the replica stands at the same address in the village.

The village's imaginary residents buy their goods at the Waterford general store and attend special occasions at the Clinton Inn, both brought here from nearby small towns. For entertainments and civic meetings they assemble at the Town

Hall and on Sundays gather at the opposite end of the Green in the Martha-Mary Chapel. It is a life that contains many of the benefits of the machine age, but none of its drawbacks. It is America in that moment of suspension between future and past that Henry Ford felt was the pinnacle of its history.

There are several ways to get around the village. Carriage rides are available all year. In the summer months and on spring and fall weekends, a steam train circles the area. A steamboat puffs around Suwanee Park and Model Ts chug through the streets. Best of all, in winter there are sleigh rides through the snow-covered village streets. Then if ever, with the crowds gone and a silent mantle of white on the ground, Greenfield Village looks exactly as its creator had intended.

The adjacent Henry Ford Museum shares this ambivalence toward machines. Its central exhibit hall covers eight acres and 200 years of industrial science. Every conceivable machine that plays a part in our lives—from stoves to vacuum cleaners to phonographs to airplanes to automobiles—is on display here, from its first crude model to its final refined form. It is fascinating to trace the development of something like the washing machine, looking at the first uncertain attempts to harness machinery for the housewife and then following the improvements to the sleek, multispeed, rinse-cycled marvels of today. The automotive section is excellent, as you would expect. It is logically laid out, too, with steamers grouped in one section, electric cars in another. Attention is paid to chronology, so that the styling changes are clearly apparent across the years. The exhibits are also clearly and lucidly marked.

But adjoining this massive hall is the Street of Early American Shops, in which specially trained craftsmen practice the skills that disappeared from American life because machines could produce the goods faster and cheaper. The museum also contains several galleries of decorative arts, room settings from various areas and eras of American history. Three second-floor galleries contain a personal history of Ford.

He died in 1947 in his nearby estate, Fair Lane. It was a death the old man might have arranged for himself. The banks of the Rouge River, a stream he made synonymous with industrial power, had overflown in spring storms and cut off the power supply to the house. He died by candlelight in a wood-heated room, in exactly the sort of setting the machine age had swept away.

Greenfield Village is open from 9:00 to 6:00 in summer; 9:00 to 5:00 in winter; 9:00 to 5:30 weekdays in spring and fall and 9:00 to 6:00 weekends at that time. Museum hours are approximately the same; open until 6:00 on winter weekends. There is an admission charge to each.

A sleigh ride through the snow-covered streets of Greenfield Village evokes an America that has vanished. *Courtesy Michigan Travel Commission.*

New Center Walk

Suburbia began here, on the corner of West Grand Boulevard and Second Avenue in Detroit. Oh, we're still deep in the heart of the city. But it was at this intersection in 1921 that the burgeoning General Motors Corporation began scouting the frontier of an intriguing new idea. Was it possible to have an alternative to downtown?

Until then, the question hardly had been considered. There could be only one central business district. Rail and trolley lines converged on it and then carried passengers away again to their homes in the new neighborhoods which had sprung up along their tracks.

But by its second decade of general use, the motorcar was changing everything. Residential patterns no longer were bound to rails, they could spring up anywhere, wherever a road was built. Urban living areas were becoming dispersed across a wide band of the American city. Could that also be true for working patterns?

General Motors had become the young giant of the auto industry since its formation in 1913. Within a few years it was looking for a permanent corporate headquarters in Detroit. A location away from downtown would seem to symbolize the changes that were sweeping across the country, changes stimulated by the very machines GM was building.

Grand Boulevard had been plotted in the 1890s, outlining an irregular arc along what was then the city limits. It became a fashionable address and many wealthy families put up imposing homes along its length. By the 1920s, though, Detroit had grown far beyond these limits and the Boulevard (as it is still called) was in residential decline. At its northern perimeter, it was two and a half miles from downtown. GM picked a site one block west of its intersection with the city's main street, Woodward Avenue, and began to build. The surrounding area was immediately named The New Center.

GM commissioned architect Albert Kahn to create its new home. Kahn had virtually invented the modern factory. He pioneered the use of glass and steel construction in a plant built for the Burroughs Corporation in 1904. It had more light and ventilation than any previous factory building and, most important, vast amounts of space under one roof. That factory corresponded to the sort of facility envisioned by Henry Ford as he prepared to go into assembly-line production of automobiles. He hired Kahn to design his landmark Highland Park plant, the first automotive mass-production factory. He turned again to Kahn when it came time to expand into the massive River Rouge complex with its totally integrated manufacturing processes. Building B, the nucleus of the Rouge, was opened in 1920. Now, a year later, Kahn had a chance to display his work in a public building.

At its completion, the GM Building was the second largest office structure in the world. A vast structure, occupying an entire city block, it is an almost perfect reflection of the business that it houses. Shaped like a massive hollow square, it has the appearance of an impregnable fortress. There is nothing lovely about it. It represents power, machinery, production. Look at the repeating rows of windows and columns down the length of the entire front. There is a hypnotizing force about them, like the strength of an automobile assembly line. The facade had to be moved back, intact, when the Boulevard was widened, but it lost none of its force. Its huge first-floor showrooms remain the best place in the city to check out the new line of GM cars.

Across the Boulevard is another Kahn masterpiece, the Fisher Building, showing another side of his skill. This skyscraper was the second major installation in the New Center, built in 1928. Although it is only thirty stories high, it appears much taller because of its detached location and Kahn's use of setbacks to accentuate the vertical lines of the soaring central tower.

Walk inside to take a look at the interior decoration, especially the ceiling mosaics in the main lobby. They're worth a climb to the mezzanine balcony for a closer inspection. The building houses several shops, as well as the city's major legitimate theatre, the Fisher Theatre. In its use of enclosed shopping concourses, it anticipated the contemporary suburban mall by three decades. It is also connected by a tunnel to the GM Building, and the shops at this subterranean level were another

New Center Walk

1   General Motors Building
2   Fisher Building
3   New Center One
4   New Center Commons
5   Burroughs Corporation Building
6   McGregor Memorial Conference Center
7   College of Education
8   Detroit Public Library
9   Detroit Historical Museum
10 International Institute
11 Children's Museum
12 Detroit Institute of Arts
13 Detroit Science Center

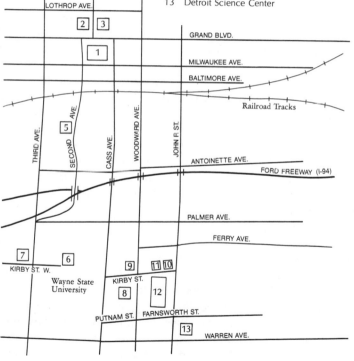

first in American urban planning. The entire complex was studied and used as a model by the planners of New York's Rockefeller Center a few years later.

A new office building, New Center One, finished in 1982, completes the main grouping at the intersection. A series of elevated glass skywalks bridge the streets to connect it with both the Fisher and GM Buildings. Criticized at first for disrupting the visual unity of the area, the skywalks have become a popular part of the New Center scene. The twin atriums and huge suspended sculptures in New Center One are worth a walk in the sky.

In the blocks north of this area, GM is underwriting an enormous experiment in urban redevelopment, New Center Commons. Entire blocks of decaying older housing were purchased, restored, and resold to a predominantly middle-class market, while new, moderately-priced high rise apartments were also built. To get an idea of what has been done here, walk three blocks north on Second Avenue to Pallister Avenue and turn west. This striking pedestrian area, lined with dignified Victorian homes, is a landmark in the city's attempts at rebirth.

Now return to Second Avenue and start heading south. You will pass the satellite GM developments and pass under the rail viaduct that defines the southern limits of the New Center. In a few minutes you will be walking by the headquarters of the Burroughs Corporation, a contemporary structure put up over the framework of Kahn's original building. Second Avenue is a wide, divided boulevard here, and as it reaches the Edsel Ford Freeway (I-94) overpass it crosses into the Cultural Center and the borders of Wayne State University.

The university was founded in 1867, but dates its current identity from 1933, when it moved into the then-recently vacated Detroit Central High School building, a few blocks south of here at Cass and Warren avenues. From this tiny nucleus, it has grown into a sprawling midcity institution, with an enrollment of 30,000, drawn almost exclusively from the metropolitan area. In recent years, it has led all major universities in percentage of black undergraduate enrollment.

As Second Avenue begins a sweep to the west, continue to walk straight, past a lineup of parking structures. You are now entering the central university mall. If you have time for no other sightseeing, visit the McGregor Memorial Conference Center, on the east side of Second, between Kirby Street and Ferry Avenue. This delicate structure, which seems almost to float above its surrounding pools, is the work of Minoru Yamasaki, a Detroit-based architect with a national reputation. Critics complain that it fails to provide adequate kitchen and meeting facilities for a conference center and that its Oriental motif is out of place in this urban setting. Nonetheless, it remains the most popular landmark on the campus. Another example of Yamasaki's work is across Second Avenue in the College of Education building. This was somewhat less enthusiastically received, with some comparing it to an inverted wedding cake.

Walk east on Kirby Street across Cass Avenue and you'll come to the Cultural Center proper. Directly to your right is the Detroit Public Library and across Woodward Avenue, in a matching Italian Renaissance palazzo, is the Detroit Institute of Arts.

The library was the first of the two to open, in 1921. Besides being one of the largest open-shelf facilities in the country, it is noted for its Burton Historical Collection, material pertaining to the Northwest Territory and early Michigan, and its second-floor murals illustrating local history. The murals are the work of several artists, most notably Gari Melchers. The library is closed Sunday and Monday. It is open Wednesday, 1:00 to 9:00; all other days, 9:30 to 5:30.

Across Kirby Street is the Detroit Historical Museum. Its first-floor exhibit rooms feature a variety of changing displays and its Streets of Old Detroit section re-creates actual storefronts from various periods of the city's history, complete with genuine artifacts and guides in period dress who give various demonstrations. Hours vary, but it is generally open Tuesday to Saturday, 9:30 to 5:00. A donation is requested.

Before entering the Detroit Institute of Arts, take a short detour north along Woodward Avenue to Ferry Street. In the last quarter of the nineteenth century, this part of the city saw

Victorian ostentation reach its highest level. Take a look, as an example, at the Hecker Mansion, now occupied by the Smiley Brothers Music Company, at the northeast corner of Woodward and Ferry. Built in 1890, this miniature French chateau was a showplace of the vanished, pre-automotive city. In its full-sized ballroom on the second floor, the Heckers celebrated the marriage of their daughter into the Austro-Hungarian nobility. The entire block of Ferry Street between Woodward Avenue and John R Street is lined with similar, if less exalted, homes of that gilded era. It is the only such grouping surviving in Detroit, yet it barely escaped the wrecking ball when a Wayne State campus expansion plan was voted down in 1982.

Return south on John R Street to Kirby Street and turn right. On the northern side of the street are the International Institute and Children's Museum. In the 1930s, Detroit had the highest percentage of foreign-born residents of any American city and it still prides itself on its diverse ethnic mix. The International Institute celebrates Detroit's ethnicity, with displays relating to the city's multicultural makeup. Its staff will help you track down any activities going on in various ethnic communities. The Children's Museum next door has interesting displays of African art and Michigan wildlife. It is open Monday to Friday, 1:00 to 4:00 and on Saturday during the school year, from 9:00 to 4:00. A donation is requested.

The main entrance to the Art Institute is right across the street. Enlarged many times since its opening in 1927, the museum is regarded as one of the country's best, especially with its world class collection of Italian Renaissance painting. Two of its more notable recent acquisitions are Titian's *Man with a Flute* and Caravaggio's *Conversion of the Magdalene.*

Its most famous room, however, is the Central Court, with its murals of industry by Diego Rivera. Commissioned by the institute's wealthy patrons, the murals touched off a local furor when they were unveiled in 1931. Rivera's outspoken sympathy for the workers led the sponsors to believe they were being ridiculed in the murals and a few of the more sensitive ones accused the artist of engaging in communist provocation at their expense. They are now among the city's best-loved cultural treasures. The institute's Garden Court is a fine luncheon stop. The museum is open Tuesday through Sunday, 9:30 to 5:30. A donation is requested.

The latest addition to the Cultural Center grouping is the Detroit Science Center, a block south of the Art Institute, on John R Street at Warren Avenue. A special project of the Ferry family (you walked down the street named for them a little while ago), the Center is still expanding. Its most popular attraction is its domed theater featuring 360-degree films. It is open Tuesday through Friday, 9:00 to 4:00; Saturday, 10:00 to 8:30 and Sunday, noon to 8:30. There is an admission charge.

A Walk in Downtown Detroit

Detroit owes its existence to the river. Its founder arrived on the Detroit River, the city grew because of its position on the river, and it became a metropolis because of the cheap transportation for its products on the river. Then for a century Detroit ignored its river. For a time, in the prosperous 1920s, there were vague plans for developing the riverfront. But they were put aside, and when the boom times ended in 1929, they were out of the question.

At the close of World War II, the Detroit waterfront was a tangle of nondescript buildings, forlorn warehouses, and teetering docks. The river might as well have been a thousand miles away for all the connection it had to downtown Detroit. But now the city has come full circle. The riverfront has been developed for the full breadth of the central business district and the hopes of the entire city hinge upon these projects.

So any walk through downtown Detroit must begin at the river. As good a place to start as any is the foot of Woodward Avenue, the city's main street. It is named after Judge Augustus Woodward who planned the city's rebuilding after the fire of 1805. The sly old judge always claimed, however, that the street was so named because it ran toward the woods—or wood-ward. The new Hart Plaza begins where Woodward ends. This vast, open space has become the city's central gathering place, a spot for river watching in one direction and skyline gazing in the other. On summer weekends ethnic festivals are held here, and in winter the skating rink on the lower level becomes a hub of activity. The plaza, named for the late U.S. Senator Philip Hart, is situated around the Dodge Fountain, a bequest to the city by the widow of the automaker. The computer-operated fountain, with its design reminiscent of an automobile's piston, won mixed reviews from local art critics, but it's a unanimous favorite on warm, summer nights among the plaza crowds. Across Jefferson Avenue on the right is Detroit's City-County Building, opened in 1957. The sculpture in front is officially known as *The Spirit of Detroit* but everyone calls it the Jolly Green Giant. Across Woodward Avenue is the graceful

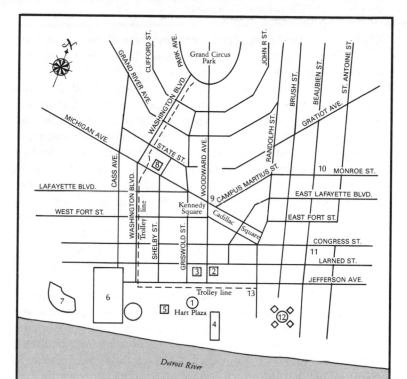

1   Dodge Fountain
2   City-County Building
3   Michigan Consolidated Gas Company Building
4   Ford Auditorium
5   Veterans' Memorial
6   Cobo Hall
7   Joe Louis Arena
8   Book Cadillac Hotel
9   Soldiers and Sailors Monument
10 Greektown
11 Bricktown
12 Renaissance Center
13 Mariners Church

Downtown Detroit

Michigan Consolidated Gas Company, one of several striking buildings in the Detroit area designed by nationally known architect Minoru Yamasaki, who lives in Detroit.

Walk down to the water to take a look at Windsor across the river. It is a truly rare vista, the only point in the United States at which you can look south to Canada. The building on your left along the riverfront is the Ford Auditorium. Opened in 1956 as the home of the Detroit Symphony Orchestra, it was a gift to the city from the Ford Motor Company. The structure on the right is the Veterans' Memorial Building, a conference center that was the first of the new riverfront structures, opened in 1950. It stands at approximately the spot at which Cadillac and his band came ashore in 1701 to found the city. Marshall Fredericks, the sculptor who fashioned the Jolly Green Giant, also did the thirty-foot high eagle on the front of the Memorial Building.

The westernmost buildings in the Civic Center grouping are Cobo Hall and Convention Arena, and beyond that, the Joe Louis Arena, first opened for the Republican National Convention of 1980. These facilities make Detroit one of the country's top convention cities and, in addition, are the sites of concerts, trade shows, and sports events all year round.

If you return to Jefferson, you can catch the trolley for a short ride through the business district. These little streetcars were imported from Portugal in 1976 and run the length of the business district, from the Renaissance Center to Grand Circus Park, for the fare of a quarter. The car ascends a gentle incline as it starts off, all that remains of Savoyard Creek, once a major geographic feature of the city but now completely paved over. This area was just beyond the western limits of the eighteenth-century British fort here. The northern boundary is delineated by Fort Street, now the main street of Detroit's financial district. Next is Lafayette Boulevard, home address of both of the city's daily newspapers. Even dearer to the hearts of Detroiters are the tiny restaurants serving Coney Island hot dogs and hamburgers, a spicy fast food concoction that is a local institution. They are clustered one block east of the trolley line. Once past Lafayette Boulevard, the trolley enters Washington Boulevard proper. At one time the location of the city's most fashionable shops and hotels, the wide boulevard has slowly declined in recent years. The Book Cadillac Hotel, at Michigan Avenue, opened in 1926 as the growing city's showplace. It was saved from closing by an extraordinary civic rescue effort in 1980 and has been nicely refurbished in its public areas. Its rival from the past, the former Statler, sits abandoned, however, a few blocks to the north, at Park Avenue. Plans to reopen it as a residential development were announced in 1984.

Grand Circus Park, a circular pigeon-dappled plaza is the end of the trolley line. Judge Woodward envisioned it as the site of the state capitol; now it merely marks the northern end of the business district. Swing around the corner on the right and you are back on Woodward Avenue. Once the main shopping street of Detroit, this is another area that has undergone sad decline in recent years. The enormous J. L. Hudson Company department store, once the second largest in the country, was shut down in 1983, the victim of its own offspring found scattered throughout suburban malls. But many smaller busi-nesses remain on the street, including the original of the now national chain of S. S. Kresge stores.

At Michigan Avenue you enter Kennedy Square, a summer-time hangout for alfresco lunchers and other assorted characters. Cross Woodward Avenue to the left of the Soldiers and Sailors Monument, a landmark here since 1872. The area to its right is Cadillac Square, historic heart of the city, now defaced by a bus terminal. The wide street to the left is Campus Martius, which leads into Monroe Street. Follow Monroe until it narrows and walk for two more blocks. You are now in Greektown, a block-long Hellenic festival that is one of downtown's sprightli-est corners. The street is lined with good, inexpensive restaurants, European style groceries, bakeries, and coffeehouses. Uniformed policemen and detectives from Police Headquarters just around the corner sit next to ancient men and college students in bustling places like the New Hellas, Laikon, and Grecian Gardens. It is one of the most intensive concentrations of Greek cuisine in the country. Stop in for a bite or just take out some baklava to nibble on as you stroll.

Turn right on St. Antoine Street. The streets running north from the river in this area still bear the names of the French farmers whose land they now run over. It is one of the city's few mementoes of its French past. This area of the city is known as Bricktown and is combed with older commercial buildings that, under the impetus of the Renaissance Center a few blocks away, have been converted into restaurants and entertainment places. You'll find them along the length of the area bounded by St. Antoine Street, Brush Street, Jefferson Avenue, and Fort Street. At Jefferson Avenue, turn right and you will be face to face with Renaissance Center, the $337 million development on the river. Designed by architect John Portman, Ren Cen includes a seventy-story hotel, the Detroit Westin, tallest building in Michigan. It is flanked by four thirty-nine-story office towers and shopping arcades. In the branch of the National Bank of Detroit in Tower 200 is the Money Museum, a unique exhibit on the history of currency. Some of the oldest, most unusual and most beautiful samples of legal tender in the world are displayed here. Best of all, the Money Museum is absolutely free. Open banking days, from 9:00 to 4:30.

Before entering this incredible complex and ascending to the Westin's revolving summit for an unequalled view of city and river, walk one block past the Center and enter the tiny church at 170 East Jefferson Avenue. This is the Mariners Church, dating from 1849, the oldest stone church in the city. It was founded with money left by two sisters who specifically willed a church meant for sailors. The interior is filled with nautical imagery. The bell is tolled here whenever a sailor is lost on the Lakes. Dwarfed by the overpowering presence of its new neighbor, Mariners Church is a continuing reminder to Detroit of the heritage it ignored for so long and now hopes desperately to regain.

Other Things to See

[1]   Michigan almost went to war with the state of Ohio in 1836 over the strip of land occupied by Toledo. There was much mustering of militia, muttered threats, and marching back and forth until President Jackson told everyone to cut it out and settle the thing peacefully. Ohio was given Toledo, and Michigan received the entire Upper Peninsula as a consolation prize. Because of the way the boundary was drawn, though, one little piece of Michigan juts defiantly into Lake Erie, accessible only from Ohio. You can catch a glimpse of the so-called Lost Peninsula, a relic of this strange affair, just as you cross into Michigan on Interstate 75.

[2]   General George Armstrong Custer may be a figure of controversy or downright derision in other parts of the country, but in Monroe, Michigan, the old Indian-fighter is a hero forever. He married local girl Elizabeth Bacon and lived in the town for various periods of his life until the Civil War. The County Historical Museum, at 126 South Monroe Street, has the country's largest collection of Custer memorabilia, including the general's desk and robe. Other exhibits trace local history. Open May through September, Tuesday through Sunday, 10:00 to 5:00, rest of year, Thursday through Sunday; free. An equestrian statue of Custer overlooks the River Raisin, three blocks north of the museum.

[3]   American troops suffered one of their bloodiest defeats in the War of 1812 along the river outside Monroe, which was then known as Frenchtown. A force on its way to try and retake Detroit in 1813 was ambushed and cut to pieces by British and Indians. Survivors of the battle were then massacred, providing American forces in the west a rallying cry for the duration of the war. A plaque marks the spot of the massacre on the river's northern bank, at Elm and North Dixie streets.

[4]   Two bridges connect the residential island of Grosse Ile to the mainland. One of the wealthiest suburbs in the area, Grosse Ile has retained the air of a country village although adjacent to some of Detroit's heaviest industrial installations. Cadillac camped on the island the night before he moved back

upstream to found Detroit. The waterfront drives command lovely views of the Detroit River and its traffic.

[5]   Fort Wayne is a fine specimen of a military installation from the Civil War period, although the old fort, at 6053 West Jefferson Avenue in Detroit, never came close to firing a shot in anger. It was garrisoned until World War II and now its limestone barracks, tunnels, and casemates are part of a military museum operated by the Detroit Historical Society. Open Wednesday through Sunday, 9:30 to 5:00, May through September. Admission charge.

[6]   Surrounded by a 70-acre nature preserve, Fair Lane, a fifty-six-room mansion built by Henry Ford in 1915 contains personal items belonging to the Ford family. It is just northwest of Greenfield Village, at 4901 Evergreen Road, Dearborn. Open Monday through Friday and Sunday, 1:00 to 4:30; admission charge.

[7]   The best way to watch the traffic on the Detroit River— busiest inland waterway in the world—is to ride the gingerbread riverboats to Bob-Lo Island, an amusement park on the Canadian side of the river at the mouth of Lake Erie. Detroiters have been taking the cruise for generations. The boats leave daily, and at night as well, from the docks at the foot of Third Street, from Memorial Day to Labor Day. Call for rates and schedule.

[8]   Hamtramck is a Polish island surrounded by the sea of Detroit. The little enclave of a city has become nationally famous, primarily for its ethnic makeup. It has changed some in recent years but still bears the imprint of its founders. Walk up its main street, Joseph Campau, to get a feeling for Hamtramck. The family store and personalized service are very much alive here. As you browse, stop in for a bite at Under the Eagle or Yemans for some stick-to-the-ribs cooking; or grab some pastries at the New Palace Bakery.

[9]   An even livelier operation is the Detroit Eastern Market, just north of Gratiot and east of downtown. It is a sprawling, brightly decorated assemblage of goods fresh from the country set down amid shops purveying all sorts of oddments, from peanuts to Syrian delicacies. Saturday morning is the busiest time.

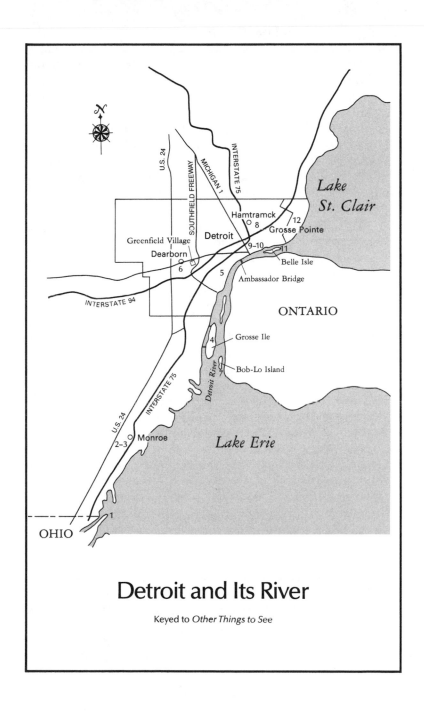

Detroit and Its River

Keyed to *Other Things to See*

[10]   Just a few blocks from the market is the Stroh's Brewery. This beer, whose popularity formerly was limited to Michigan, has spread rapidly across the Midwest and South in recent years and in some areas attained a cult status rivaling Coors of Colorado. Strohs also has become one of the country's largest brewers by acquiring the Milwaukee-based Schlitz Company. Tours are given Monday through Friday, 10:00 to 3:00, on the hour, with tastings afterwards in the Strohhaus. The entrance is at Gratiot and the Chrysler Freeway (I-75) service drive.

[11]   Belle Isle, Detroit's mid-river park, once was called Hog Island by the unromantic settlers. The 1,000-acre island is connected to the city by a bridge at East Jefferson Avenue and East Grand Boulevard. A scenic drive makes a complete loop, showing off views of the Detroit skyline, Canada, and the head of Lake St. Clair. There is a small beach on the island, as well as a nine-hole golf course, a bandshell for summer concerts, and complete recreational facilities. In the more remote center of the island there is even a herd of deer. There is also a conservatory, a fine freshwater aquarium, a children's zoo, and Dossin Great Lakes Museum, which features the hydroplane *Miss Pepsi* along with historical displays. The museum is open Wednesday through Sunday, 10:00 to 5:45. Donation asked.

[12]   Grosse Pointe is synonymous with established money and this famous group of suburbs on Detroit's northeastern border has a national reputation for the automotive world's good life. Following East Jefferson Avenue and then Lake Shore Drive is the best way to catch a glimpse of the "Pointes." With the lake on one side and the stunning homes of the industry's founding families on the other, it is one of the finest drives in the Detroit area.

Side Trips

The University of Michigan is the oldest and one of the largest state institutions of higher learning in the country. Founded in Detroit in 1817, the university moved 42 miles west to Ann Arbor in 1837. Although that city is one of the wealthiest and fastest growing in the state, it has retained a certain Ivy League air that blends nicely with its Midwestern setting in the area around its campus. Tours of the sprawling education facility are available by calling (313) 764-7268. Ann Arbor holds a week-long Art Fair each summer, usually in mid-July.

State Parks on the Lake

Sterling State Park—4 miles east of Monroe, has a history of beach problems caused by Lake Erie pollution. But there are boating and picnicking facilities there as well as 192 campsites.

There is a small beach on Belle Isle in the Detroit River which has become usable recently after an intensive cleanup campaign. There have even been a few salmon caught in the river, an unheard of event in the previously filthy stream.

The closest lake swimming to Detroit is at Metropolitan Beach, about 25 miles northeast of the city on Interstate 94. Slightly over a mile in length, the beach on Lake St. Clair is crowded on weekends but offers a nearby getaway at other times. There is a parking fee.

If you go: Spend the entire time in Detroit.

1. Take the downtown walk outlined in this chapter.
2. Take the New Center–Cultural Center walk.
3. Spend the day at Greenfield Village.
4. Drive south to the Custer Museum in Monroe, a circle drive of Grosse Ile and Fort Wayne.
5. Take a river cruise to Bob-Lo Island and spend the day there.
6. Visit the Henry Ford Museum.
7. Shop at Eastern Market—best on Saturday morning. Explore Joseph Campau Street in Hamtramck and the island park on Belle Isle.

A boardwalk snakes its way to the heart of the marsh in Point Pelee National Park, Ontario. *Courtesy the* Detroit Free Press.

Canada's Lake Erie Shore

One name keeps popping up as one drives across southwestern Ontario on Highway 3. There is Port Talbot on the lakeshore. A bit north of it is Royal Talbotville. The name of the highway itself whenever it passes through a town is Talbot Street. Even the largest city in the area, St. Thomas, is named after this Mr. Talbot. That is a nice twist, too, a fine joke on posterity, proving that Thomas Talbot was not without a sense of humor. For whatever else he was, Talbot assuredly was no saint.

The most commonly used adjective in describing him is irascible, but that might not be giving him his full due. He was an aristocrat, born into a 600-year-old barony in Malahide, Ireland. He came to Upper Canada with his regiment, served under Governor-General Simcoe, and had the opportunity to size up the best lands on expeditions to the virtually unpopulated western section of the colony. After service in the Napoleonic Wars, he returned to Canada in 1800, claiming 5,000 acres that he was entitled to by virtue of his service. He chose land at the mouth of Kettle Creek and immediately cut a deal for himself. He knew the authorities were eager to populate this area. Lying between Detroit and Niagara, it seemed especially

209

vulnerable to American invasion and the British wanted farmers on the land to secure it. There were French settlers in the Windsor area. They had been there since the 1740s, part of the old Detroit colony which had included both sides of the river before the Revolution redrew national boundaries. But their loyalty was uncertain. The British wanted their own stock to settle.

Talbot agreed to divide his holdings into fifty-acre tracts for new settlers. But as a reward, for every settler who received the land, Talbot would get an additional 200 acres for himself. By this method he expanded his holdings to 60,000 acres—12 times the original size. Not only did he win the right to increase his holdings in this fashion, but he also had absolute authority to grant his tracts to whomever he pleased. This made for some interesting situations, for Talbot, or the Colonel as he fashioned himself, was a man with definite prejudices about his settlers.

First of all, even though his own holdings depended on the arrival of the settlers, he did no recruiting. The Colonel figured that any man worth his salt would get to the land under his own steam and find him. He had a definite preference for Irishmen; it was, after all, the land of his birth. After the Irish, he had a fondness for Scots. He established himself at Port Talbot, high on a bluff above the lake, in a fine house named after his ancestral seat, Malahide. There the men with a hunger for land would meet him face-to-face and the Colonel would either deign to allow the newcomer his fifty acres or send him on his way.

Some of them did not go quietly. The story is told of one Scot who, upon hearing he did not measure up to Talbot's standards, grabbed the Colonel, flung him to the ground, and would not let him up until he got his fifty acres. Taken aback by this encounter, Talbot had a sliding half-door installed in the house. That way he could still see the supplicant plainly but at the least hint of trouble he could slide the door shut and retreat.

Talbot ruled his domain like a feudal lord but he succeeded in populating this stretch of Ontario. Talbot's holdings today comprise much of Elgin County. From the names on the land, the national origins of Talbot's hand-picked settlers live on in Wallacetown and New Glasgow and Tyrconnell; in Port Bruce and Port Burwell and Iona. Talbot's tombstone in a churchyard near Tyrconnell states simply: "Founder of the Talbot Settlement." But that was a life's work indeed.

Unlike the American shore of Lake Erie, which is dotted with large ports and important cities, Ontario's lakeshore presents an unbroken pastoral scene. The paths of commerce lead far away and Ontario's larger cities arose on the course of the railroad, several miles inland. All that remains here are a few drowsy port towns and three fingers of land that extend into the lake and have been made provincial or national parks—Point Pelee, Rondeau, and Long Point.

This is Canada's southernmost territory and very unlikely crops are grown here. The eastern counties, Elgin and Haldimand-Norfolk, are famous for tobacco fields. Especially around Simcoe the land looks more like Carolina than Canada. The western counties, Kent and Essex, are more fertile, with some of the most bounteous agricultural acres in the country. Essex, in fact, bills itself as the "Sun Parlour of Canada" and never tires of pointing out that in some locales it has the same latitude as Crescent City, California.

The largest city in this part of Ontario is Windsor. With a population of more than 200,000, it is the tenth largest city in Canada. In very few places of the world do major cities of two different countries face each other across such a narrow frontier. Although Windsor is virtually a part of Detroit's metropolitan area, it is also quite separate. There are large automobile plants in Windsor, as in Detroit, but it is more than a simple mirror image of the behemoth across the river. It has a distinct character of its own. Detroiters come here at times to get away from their problem-wracked city and recall the pleasures of strolling slower-paced streets. There are several good restaurants that draw a lively trade across the bridge and tunnel that connect the two cities. A harness track also acts as a powerful magnet. The city was at its most alluring, though, during Prohibition when dry Detroiters only had to take the ferryboat across for a drink. There was an active trade in making it even easier for them, and rum-running to isolated landings on the Michigan shore was a lively industry in the area.

Windsor, although settled shortly after Detroit, is a far newer city. It was not incorporated until 1896 and reached its present size only after extensive annexation in 1935. It has also retained its French heritage to a far greater degree than its American neighbor. Several thousand French Canadians make the city their home, and there is a French language radio and television station in the city. Large communities of more recently arrived Italians and Yugoslavs also lend the city a cosmopolitan air.

Amherstburg and Fort Malden

The United States entered the War of 1812 in the manner of a football team that has been made a four-touchdown favorite. No one really expected it would take much to topple Canada. A few quick incursions at Detroit, Niagara, and Montreal and it would be all over. The French would come over to the American side, as would the more recent immigrants from the States. The comparative handful of British troops could be mopped up in no time while Britain was occupied with Napoleon a few thousand miles away.

Then in August came the news of the fall of Detroit. The effect was electric in both countries. In Canada, General Isaac Brock became a national hero, a symbol of resistance, and even those who thought the cause was hopeless determined to stand up to the Americans. In the United States it was a shock that equalled the impact of Pearl Harbor, 129 years later. It was unbelievable. In fact, just days before it was the American troops who were threatening the other side of the border. Detroit had been well defended. The command was in the hands of General William Hull, a hero of the Revolution. There had to be treachery. There was no other explanation.

Fort Malden Historic Site in Amherstburg, 18 miles downriver from Windsor, preserves the base of the combined British and Indian force that took Detroit. The northwest earthwork bastion of the original fort remains along with a brick barracks building erected a few years after the war. The fort was constructed in 1796–99. Immediately after the British were forced to turn over Detroit to General Anthony Wayne they withdrew to this part of the river to build a new installation. It was a square-shaped affair containing eleven buildings. The town of Amherstburg grew up south of the fort and the shipyards that developed there were of primary strategic importance in the war. A museum and historic programs on the fort grounds give a good perspective to this period.

When war was declared in June, 1812, Hull and his troops, mostly drawn from Kentucky, made their way overland from Cincinnati to the wilderness outpost of Detroit. The plan was for them to cross the border immediately and take Fort Malden. But Hull made his first blunder on the way. When he reached the Maumee River he sent much of his baggage ahead by boat, which was easily plucked off by the British as it passed their base at Amherstburg. Among the prizes was a copy of Hull's campaign plans. So much for the element of surprise.

In late July, Hull crossed into Canada. Instead of moving on the lightly defended Malden, though, he made his second mistake. He hesitated. An advance guard got into a skirmish with British troops but no other contact was made. Finally, Hull returned to Detroit without accomplishing anything.

Meanwhile, the situation was changing rapidly. Brock had made his way along Lake Erie's northern shore to assume command at Fort Malden. Far to the north, Fort Michilimackinac, key to the upper lakes, had fallen to the British and a large Indian force began moving south to link up with Brock. Also joining Brock was Tecumseh, the great Shawnee chief, who had threatened the Indiana frontier until his defeat at Tippecanoe the year before. The far-sighted Tecumseh realized the British were his only hope to stop the relentless onrush of white settlers onto his land. He pledged his aid to Brock on the grounds of Fort Malden.

On August 15, Brock arrived opposite Detroit and began cannonading the Americans. The next day he crossed the river to the south of the village and prepared to settle in for a siege. In a matter of hours Hull surrendered without firing a shot. He explained afterward that he was horrified at the prospect of a massacre of Detroit's civilian population by the Indians if he resisted, fears deliberately fed by the British. Actual slaughters would take place during the war at Fort Dearborn, Frenchtown, and Black Rock; the British deploring them each time but explaining that their allies were Indians, after all, and boys will be boys. Hull's junior officers were mortified. Many testified against him at a court-martial after prisoners were exchanged. Hull was found not guilty because of his previous military record but lived out his days in disgrace.

The British, meanwhile, with a secure base at Amherstburg raided freely along the western shore of Lake Erie. Brock was called away to the Niagara frontier and died at Queenston Heights, two months after Detroit fell. After Commodore Perry's naval victory at Put-in-Bay the following summer, the British position became untenable. Over Tecumseh's vigorous protests, they began to retreat across Canada, hoping to reach Niagara. But the American forces caught them at Thamesville and in a savage battle annihilated the British. Among the slain was Tecumseh.

In addition to the remains of the riverside fort, Amherstburg contains other fine old buildings. Just south of Fort Malden, the site of the old shipyards has been excavated and turned into a riverside park. Many of the structures in the immediate area date from the 1840s, including the old Salmoni Hotel at Dalhousie and Richmond streets. It now houses a pleasant restaurant, The Old Navy Yard. Also on the edge of the park is the Park House, built in 1796 on the Michigan side of the river and floated piecemeal across the water to its present location by its ardently Loyalist owner. It is now a museum of the town. It is open daily, June through August, 10:00 to 5:00; September through December 21, Tuesday to Friday, 12:30 to 4:30; March 21 through May, Sundays only, 1:30 to 4:30. There is an admission charge.

Turn left at Gore Street, repaved in brick and lined with antique lights. Facing each other at the western side of Ramsey Street are two of the oldest houses in town; the John Askin House on the south and the Berthelot House on the north. Both date from around 1830. A bit further down Ramsey is Christ Church, oldest in the area, built in 1818 and used by the Fort Malden garrison.

Amherstburg was a place of refuge for escaped slaves before the American Civil War and that era is commemorated in the North American Black Cultural Centre, on King Street just south of Gore. It adjoins the Nazrey A.M.E. Church, built in 1848, and illustrates with displays and artifacts the history of that era.

South of town on Highway 18 are the docks of the ferry to Bob-Lo Park, an island facility that may also be reached by boat from downtown Detroit (see chapter 8). Along the river road, you will pass Belle Vue, a neoclassical mansion built in 1818 by trade commissioner Robert Reynolds. His wife's family made a fortune in the fur trade and he sank much of it into this house. Now owned by St. Nicholas Ukrainian Church, it is closed to the public but visible from the road.

Fort Malden, now entirely surrounded by the town, was garrisoned until 1851 by the British. It was demilitarized completely seven years later and became a lunatic asylum. The land was acquired by the government in 1939 and has been a museum since then. It is open daily, from 10:00 to 5:00; free.

Point Pelee

National parks usually are scenic exclamation points. They stun you with soaring mountains, awe you with yawning canyons, overwhelm you with caves or waterfalls or silent forests. Point Pelee does none of these things. The adjective most frequently applied to the park, in fact, is fragile, like the imported china on sale in the shops of nearby Windsor. But the Canadian national park has a subtle charm of its own that works a slow but certain spell on those who linger.

One park superintendent stationed there in recent years found that almost in spite of himself he was falling under its enchantment. "My two assignments before this one were in Jasper in the Rockies and on Vancouver Island. My family was kind of accustomed to wide open spaces and we weren't used to the idea of stepping out the front door into someone's tomato patch. But after a while you start to realize what is here. The lake and the marsh, the incredible variety of plants and animals, the human history of the area. You start adding it up and you understand."

The park is barely an hour's drive from the tumult of the Detroit-Windsor area. On summer weekends the crowds from the city pour into its 4,000 acres. Cottages crowd right up to the park line and, in a few cases, spill over onto park territory. When the Point became a national park in 1918, much of it was in the hands of private landowners. The government has managed to buy out all but a handful of them. In self-defense, the park has instituted the most rigorous protective measures in the Canadian park system. During the summer, automobiles are banned from the Point itself, the southern extremity of the slender finger that juts into the lake toward Ohio. Visitors must park their cars at the Nature Center and board a propane-fueled tractor train for an eight-minute ride to the Point. Access to the park also is closed after electronic counting devices at the entry gate tally a certain number.

Some of the attractions on this southernmost part of the Canadian mainland are not only unique, but also, given the proximity of such a large industrialized urban complex, almost astonishing. Because of Lake Erie's temperate climatic influence, prickly pear cactus grows here and produces brilliant yellow flowers in June and July, as in the deserts of the Southwest. The 2,500-acre freshwater marsh, one of the largest in North America, can be explored along a boardwalk that snakes for two-thirds of a mile into its heart. Pelee is a product of retreating Ice-Age glaciers which deposited sand on a lake ridge as they withdrew to the North. The marsh formed from lake water that was trapped behind the ridge and cut off from Lake Erie at that time.

The Point itself is a windswept land's end, a brooding waterscape reminiscent of the Carolina Outer Banks. Offshore currents are treacherous and swimming and wading are not permitted. But there are 14 miles of broad sand beach in other areas throughout the park.

Pelee abounds with uncommon animals, many of them members of the endangered species list. The fox snake grows to a length of seven feet and the rare eastern mole thrives there. But it is the winged life, the birds and butterflies, that give Point Pelee its worldwide reputation among ornithologists and entomologists. The park checklist shows 336 species of birds that have been sighted here, although some, like the Bohemian waxwing, have not been seen since 1911. During the great spring and fall migrations, even those whose bird identification capability is limited to red-winged blackbirds, turn out at dawn to hear the avian chorus of the resting flocks. Point Pelee lies on one of the continent's great migratory routes and 90 species stay there all season long to nest.

Just as spectacular is the passage of the monarch butterflies. They range over the entire eastern half of the United States and Canada, and, like the birds, employ Point Pelee as a convenient flyway to the South. There are two annual migrations, but the bigger one comes in the fall, usually in late September and early October. The new generation born during the summer augments the numbers as the butterflies make their return trip to the southern winter grounds.

Pelee was a well-known landmark to early explorers. The two priests, Dollier and Galinee, who explored the lake's northern shore in 1669, lost their provisions and altar on its beach when a sudden storm swept them away. A British relief force, trying to break Pontiac's siege of Detroit in 1763, was ambushed on the beach and sixty men were killed. General Brock and his troops camped here in 1812 on their way to Fort Malden and another siege of Detroit.

The point today is not much changed from those years. On a bright spring morning a stroller along the marsh boardwalk, surrounded by rustling cattails and the calls of hidden birds, can easily forget that a great city lies just beyond the horizon, its presence marked only by a faint smudge on the sky. One hour and another world away.

The Birdman of Kingsville

On an April morning in 1908, Jack Miner left his farmhouse to inspect the pond on his land, outside Kingsville, Ontario. It was something of a ritual with him. He had been making this inspection trip for the last four years, through late October and November in the autumn, and then again in April the next spring. Always, he was disappointed. He hoped that wild Canada geese would stop at the pond at the end of their long flight across Lake Erie en route to their summer grounds near Hudson Bay. Miner's land lay along one of the great bird migration routes in the world and the geese passed over twice a year on their seasonal journeys. Of course, that was not clearly understood then. The migration patterns of the geese had never been fully or accurately traced. That was to be the great work that Miner accomplished. All he knew was that the geese came over and that their numbers were declining alarmingly with each year. He wanted to make his pond their sanctuary.

In the autumn of 1904 he purchased seven geese whose wings had been clipped and placed them near the pond. He persuaded nearby farmers not to shoot at the passing flocks. His hope was that passing geese would see others of their kind living unmolested and that in some mysterious manner the concept of safe landing would spread through the flocks. But the years went by and no birds came. They passed in the skies but never landed. His neighbors, interested at first in this curious experiment, started to laugh at Miner. A few of the more fun-loving souls took to greeting him with "Honk! Honk!"

But on the morning of April 1, 1908, there were 11 new birds at the pond. They stayed the spring. Miner, rewarding his neighbors for their cooperation, permitted them to shoot some of the birds. The rest took off for the North and Miner spent the rest of the year wondering what would happen the next spring. His answer came in March. Thirty-two geese came and stayed at the pond. In 1910 they returned, 400 strong, and in 1911 they came by the thousands.

Today the Jack Miner Bird Sanctuary is one of the continent's most unforgettable sights. The summer traveler will be disappointed because the grounds are open only from mid-October to mid-April. But if you are in the area off-season, particularly at the peak of migration (roughly the two weeks on either side of April 1 and November 1) make an effort to see it. The spectacle of these great birds covering the fields around the old Miner farm, or soaring overhead in honking flocks that fill the sky, is something you will keep with you always. The Stuart Playfair Nature Center, built with the bequest of a Toronto family, overlooks the present version of Miner's pond. In former years, visitors to the sanctuary would climb up an old tower in order to view the flocks. Now you can take a bleacher seat in this new facility. The best time to watch the flocks is an hour before dusk, but a fly-over of birds already arrived on the grounds is arranged at about 3:30 P.M. each day.

After Miner's initial success in attracting the flocks he began to wonder about the instincts that guided them unfailingly to his sanctuary. He attached address bands to the legs of the geese and ducks that rested on his grounds with a Biblical verse usually scratched upon it. Over the years reports began coming back to Kingsville, from South America to Hudson Bay. Miner put up a large map and placed dots on every location in which one of his banded windfowl was shot by a hunter. Soon he was able to construct a chart of the migration paths of the birds. He could see how they came down from the North and then dispersed across the South once they traversed Lake Erie. It was a chart that encompassed half a continent. And yet every spring and fall the birds would find their way back to Miner's land. What more appropriate piece of writing to accompany such a miraculous voyage than a verse from the Bible?

As word of Miner's success spread, his sanctuary became famous. Henry Ford became a major sponsor. The baseball player Ty Cobb came out to visit from Detroit and through him the Yawkey family, owners for many years of the Detroit and Boston teams, contributed generously to Miner's work. By the time of his death in 1944, Miner's efforts had been crowned with awards and medals in plenitude, including the Order of the British Empire.

His greatest reward, though, was to see the flocks of wild

Canada geese multiplying through the years. Miner estimated at one point that his sanctuary was responsible for increasing their population by 25,000 birds each year. He never opposed hunting. All he wanted was an even break for the birds. His personality is still strongly stamped upon the sanctuary. As he wished, it is closed on Sunday and no souvenirs are sold on the grounds. "Let there be at least one place on God's earth where no money changes hands," he said. That is the philosophy that remains in effect there. And his fields are filled with geese.

Flocks of Canada geese fill the sky during migration season at Jack Miner's Bird Sanctuary near Kingsville, Ontario. *Courtesy Ontario Ministry of Industry and Tourism.*

Other Things to See

[1]   Riverside Drive offers pleasant vistas of the Detroit River, Belle Isle, and the American city across the river as it passes through some of Windsor's nicest residential neighborhoods and parks, east of the business district.

[2]   Walkerville used to be a separate community before joining with other towns in the area to form Windsor in 1935. In the shadow of the Hiram Walker Distillery (Canadian Club) it is still a handsome neighborhood with well-maintained turn-of-the-century homes. The section around St. Mary's Anglican Church, at Niagara and Kildare streets, is especially pleasant for strolling. Nearby is spacious Willistead Park. The Willistead Mansion, within its confines, is now a public library branch. Tours of the Hiram Walker plant are given at 10:00 and 2:00 on weekdays during the summer.

[3]   Windsor and Detroit are connected by an international tunnel and bridge. The tunnel joins the business districts of the two cities, between Renaissance Center and Ouellette, Windsor's main street. The Ambassador Bridge, 1 mile downriver, offers a route that bypasses the hearts of the cities and some fine views of the two skylines.

[4]   An even better view of Detroit's wall of skyscrapers can be seen from Windsor's Dieppe Gardens on the riverfront. Windsor, in contrast to its neighbor across the river, turned over its water frontage to parkland long ago. The result is a lovely urban park with some of the most dramatic vistas in the area.

[5]   When William Hull and his Kentuckians crossed the river in 1812 in their abortive move on Fort Malden, the headquarters of the American staff was the home of Francois Baby. It is the oldest brick house still standing along the river and was handsomely restored by the Hiram Walker Foundation. The Baby House now is Windsor's Historical Museum with artifacts from several periods in the city's past. It faces the river across Riverside Drive from the Dieppe Gardens. Open Tuesday through Saturday, from 9:00 to 5:00; Sunday, 2:00 to 5:00; free.

[6]   The Art Gallery of Windsor contains an outstanding assortment of Eskimo art, with its mystic renderings of owls and other northern creatures. There are also galleries with collec-

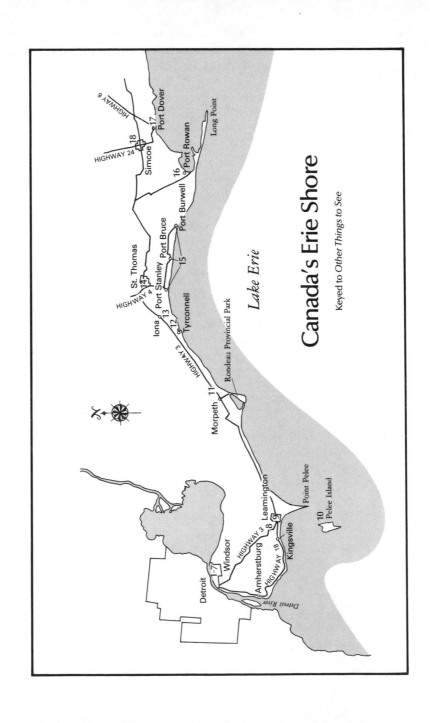

Canada's Erie Shore

Keyed to *Other Things to See*

Lake Erie

Detroit River

Detroit
Windsor
Amherstburg
Leamington
Kingsville
Point Pelee
Pelee Island
Morpeth
Tyrconnell
Rondeau Provincial Park
Iona
Port Stanley
Port Bruce
St. Thomas
Port Burwell
Port Rowan
Port Dover
Simcoe
Long Point

HIGHWAY 6
HIGHWAY 24
HIGHWAY 4
HIGHWAY 3
HIGHWAY 3
HIGHWAY 8
HIGHWAY 18

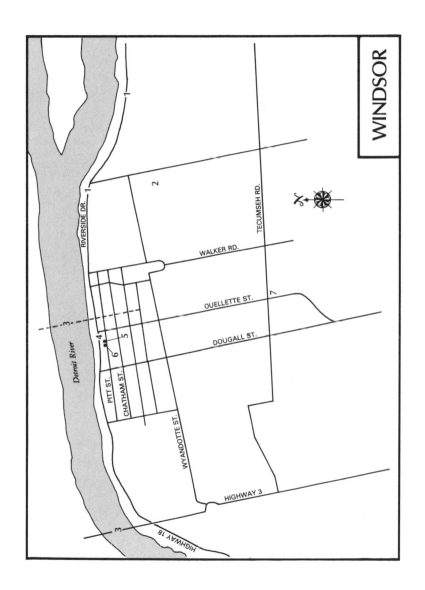

WINDSOR

Detroit River

RIVERSIDE DR.

WALKER RD.

OUELLETTE ST.

DOUGALL ST.

TECUMSEH RD.

PITT ST.

CHATHAM ST.

WYANDOTTE ST.

HIGHWAY 3

HIGHWAY 18

tions of landscapes by the Group of Seven and a branch of the Royal Ontario Museum. Open Tuesday through Saturday, 10:00 to 6:00; Sunday, 1:00 to 5:00; free. It is west of the Baby House.

[7]   Jackson Park is Windsor's most elaborate, a sunken garden with statuary and fountains that are beautifully lighted at night. It is on Ouellette and Tecumseh streets, a few miles south of downtown.

[8]   Essex County is Canada's banana belt and you will see greenhouses along country roads all through the area, built to take advantage of the comparatively mild climate. Biggest of all is Colasanti's on Highway 3, just west of Ruthven. Besides a large assortment of tropical plants and shrubs, a series of interconnected greenhouses contains the largest variety of cactus plants on the continent. Open 8:00 to 4:30, Monday through Saturday; 10:00 to 4:30 on Sunday; free.

[9]   Right in front of Leamington's civic buildings sits the Big Tomato, a tribute to the big money crop around these parts. Heinz of Canada operates a plant in town and offers weekday tours. Hours vary.

[10]   Aside from its being the largest island in Lake Erie, there is not too much happening on Pelee Island, which suits its residents right down to their shoes. It is delightfully peaceful and the perfect goal for a day excursion by boat. The M.S. *Leamington* calls daily from Leamington. Schedule information is available at the mainland dock and can also be obtained by calling (519) 724-2115. The M.V. *Pelee Islander* makes summer round trips across the lake from Leamington or Kingsville to Sandusky, Ohio, with stops at Pelee Island each way.

[11]   Highway 3 runs on bluffs above the lake between Wheatley and Cedar Springs, then again from Morpeth to Eagle, which makes for a most pleasant drive. Watch for Trinity Anglican Church, built in 1845, between Morpeth and Palmyra on a lovely location above the lake.

[12]   St. Peter's Anglican Church in Tyrconnell is the final resting place of the feudal lord Thomas Talbot. His grave is in the beautiful churchyard overlooking the lake. A few miles to the east is Port Talbot. A plaque marks the location of Talbot's

estate, Malahide, now occupied by a dairy farm of the same name.

[13]   What sort of people built the double-walled village at Southwold Earthworks near Iona? The French called these Indians Neutrals, but when the first Europeans reached this part of Canada the inhabitants of this village already had departed. They grew tobacco and corn and lived here about 600 years ago. But why the double walls, the only Indian construction of its kind found in Canada? A most mysterious place.

[14]   St. Thomas was the largest city of Colonel Talbot's domain. There are elaborate floral exhibits in Pinafore Park and Waterworks Park. The first park also features rides on a nineteenth-century locomotive daily in July and August, 1:00 to 8:30; on Sunday only in the other months between mid-May and October, from 1:00 to 6:00.

[15]   A string of old ports and resort towns line the lakeshore east of St. Thomas. Port Stanley still enjoys a lively day trade in the summer, and the resort has a dramatic location in a deep valley carved by Kettle Creek. Port Bruce has nice views of the sand bluffs stretching off to the east from its lakeside park, making a pleasant setting for the restaurant in the old Rocabore Inn across the street. A steep hill crowned by a lighthouse leads to the small beach at Port Burwell.

[16]   John Backus built his mill north of Port Rowan in 1798 and it has been turning away at the same location ever since. The mill and surrounding valley now are a pioneer park, with an agricultural museum and small cemetery. A fine view of the mill and rapids opens out from the restored Backus homestead on an adjacent hill. The mill is open June through August, weekends and Wednesday, 12:00 to 7:00; on weekends only, in the other months from mid-May to October.

[17]   The prettiest port on the Erie Shore, Port Dover, also maintains the lake's largest fishing fleet at its bustling dock area. The town is noted for its restaurants serving fresh perch and whitefish, and for the community fish fries scheduled throughout the summer. A net-making shed on the docks has been turned into a museum of the Lake Erie fishing industry. Check locally for time. The city was burned by American raiders in

1814, one of the acts that brought on the burning of Washington, D.C., in retaliation. Grace Street has several fine red brick Victorian homes and from its foot there is a good view down the lake. Just east of town and north from Highway 6, a monument marks the place at which the priests Dollier and Galinee, first Europeans to ascend Lake Erie, spent the winter of 1669–70.

[18]   Simcoe is the center of Ontario's tobacco country and tours of processing plants are offered in nearby Delhi. Simcoe's twenty-three bell carillon tower was built in 1925 to honor the county's war dead. Also in town is the Eva Brook Donly Museum of Art and Antiques, a fine regional collection. Open Wednesday through Sunday, 1:30 to 5:00, mid-May to October; weekends only the rest of the year. There is an admission charge.

Side Trip
London, 17 miles north of St. Thomas, is Canada's ninth largest city and sits on the River Thames, just like its larger namesake. It is the seat of the University of Western Ontario's lovely campus and its Storybook Gardens in Springbank Park is one of Canada's top children's attractions, with fairy tale characters recreated in a garden setting. Open mid-April to mid-October. Fanshawe Pioneer Village, northeast of town, is a reconstructed pioneer settlement.

Provincial Parks on the Lake
Holiday Beach—9 miles southeast of Amherstburg, has a beach, trout pond, store, and complete picnicking facilities. There are 23 campsites.

Rondeau—6 miles south of Morpeth, is an 11,500-acre facility on one of the three peninsulas that dip down from Lake Erie's north shore. There are hiking trails, horseback riding, water-sport facilities, and a natural history museum. Rondeau has picnicking facilities and 261 campsites.

Wheatley—9 miles east of Leamington, has water-sports facilities, a beach, and campground with 167 campsites.

John E. Pearce—just east of Tyrconnell, and Port Bruce, just west of the town of the same name, are small, day-use parks with swimming and picnicking.

Iroquois Beach—just west of Port Burwell, has swimming, picnicking, and 235 campsites.

Long Point—4 miles south of Port Rowan, is another of the lake's unique observation points for migratory birds. The peninsula extends farther into the lake than any other, more than 20 miles, and is a favorite flyway for spring and autumn migrations. The park permits hunting of duck, geese, pheasant, and partridge on specified days in fall and is renowned for its bass fishing. The 848-acre park also has miles of sand beach and 129 campsites.

Turkey Point—10 miles southeast of Simcoe, has swimming, picnicking, and golf facilities, and the site of Fort Norfolk, where British troops were stationed during the War of 1812. There are also 300 campsites.

Selkirk—12 miles east of Port Dover, has swimming, picnic facilities, and 168 campsites.

Rock Point—32 miles east of Port Dover, has complete water-sports and picnic facilities and 50 campsites.

If you go for a weekend: Stay in Windsor.

1. Explore the riverfront and visit the Baby House and Art Gallery of Windsor.

2. Drive to Amherstburg and tour Fort Malden. Continue on to Kingsville to the Jack Miner Sanctuary.

3. Spend the day at Point Pelee National Park.

If you go for a week; Stay in Windsor for three nights, in St. Thomas for two, and in Simcoe for two.

1–3. Same as the weekend tour.

4. Drive east on Highway 3 with a stop at Tyrconnell and the Southwold Earthworks. Explore the parks and gardens of St. Thomas.

5. Take a side trip to London.

6. Head east along the lakeshore through the sleepy port towns. Visit the lively dock area in Port Dover and the Donly Museum in Simcoe.

7. Tour the tobacco farms and processing plant in nearby Delhi. Drive to the Backus Mill north of Port Rowan.

Bibliography

Angus, Margaret. *The Old Stones of Kingston*. Toronto: University of Toronto Press, 1966.

Baird, David M. *The National Parks in Ontario*. Ottawa: Canadian Geological Survey, 1963.

Bald, F. Clever. *Michigan in Four Centuries*. New York: Harper and Row, 1954.

Brebner, J. Bartlet. *Canada: A Modern History*. Ann Arbor: University of Michigan Press, 1970.

————. *The Explorers of North America, 1492–1806*. London: A and C Black Ltd., 1933.

Brunger, Eric, and Wyld, Lionel. *The Grand Canal; New York's First Thruway*. Buffalo and Erie County Historical Society, 1964.

Buck, Solon J., and Buck, Elizabeth Hawthorn. *The Planting of Civilization in Western Pennsylvania*. Pittsburgh: University of Pittsburgh Press, 1939.

Channing, Edward. *The Story of the Great Lakes*. New York: Macmillan, 1912.

Clune, Henry W. *Genesee River*. New York: Holt, Rinehart and Winston, 1963.

————. *The Rochester I Know*. New York: Doubleday, 1972.

Condon, George E. *Cleveland—The Best Kept Secret*. New York: Doubleday, 1967.

Conot, Robert. *American Odyssey*. New York: William Morrow and Co., 1974.

Cook, Lura Lincoln. *The War of 1812 on the Frontier*. Buffalo and Erie County Historical Society, 1961.

Dutton, Charles Judson. *Battle of Lake Erie*. New York: Longmans, Green and Co., 1935.

Fraser, Mary M. *Joseph Brant—Thayendanega*. Burlington: Halton Press, 1969.

Frohman, Charles E. *Cedar Point Yesterdays*. Columbus: Ohio Historical Society, 1969.

————. *Put-in-Bay: Its History*. Columbus: Ohio Historical Society, 1971.

————. *Sandusky's Yesterdays*. Columbus: Ohio Historical Society, 1968.

Gilpin, Alec R. *The War of 1812 in the Old Northwest*. East Lansing: Michigan State University Press, 1958.

Glazebrook, G. P. de T. *The Story of Toronto*. Toronto: University of Toronto Press, 1971.

Goodrich, Calvin. *The First Michigan Frontier*. Ann Arbor: University of Michigan Press, 1940.

Greenhill, Ralph, and Mahoney, Thomas D. *Niagara*. Toronto: University of Toronto Press, 1969.

Hamil, Frederick Coyne. *Lake Erie Baron: Story of Colonel Thomas Talbot*. Toronto: Macmillan, 1955.

Hatcher, Walter. *Lake Erie*. New York: Bobbs-Merrill, 1945.

————. *The Western Reserve*. Cleveland: World, 1966.

Havighurst, Walter. *The Long Ships Passing*. New York: Macmillan, 1953.

Hough, Jack L. *Geology of the Great Lakes*. Champaign: University of Illinois Press, 1958.

Howard, Robert West. *Thundergate: The Forts of Niagara*. Englewood Cliffs: Prentice-Hall, 1968.

Hultzen, Claud H. *Old Fort Niagara*. Buffalo: Old Fort Niagara Association, 1939.

Malkus, Alida. *Blue Water Boundary*. New York: Hastings House, 1960.

Malo, Paul. *Landmarks of Rochester and Monroe County*. Syracuse: Syracuse University Press, 1974.

McKee, Russell. *Great Lakes Country*. New York: Crowell, 1966.

Parkman, Francis. *The Pioneers of France in the New World*. Boston, 1903.

Pound, Arthur. *Lake Ontario*. New York: Bobbs-Merrill, 1945.

Richmond, John, and West, Bruce. *Around Toronto*. Toronto: Doubleday, 1969.

Scadding, Henry. *Toronto of Old*. Toronto: Oxford University Press, 1971.

Van Tassel, Charles Sumner. *Maumee Valley*. Chicago: S. J. Clarke, 1929.

WPA, Federal Writers Project. *Lake Erie Vacationland*. Cleveland, 1941.

————. *Pennsylvania Cavalcade*. Philadelphia: University of Pennsylvania Press, 1942.

————. *Rochester and Monroe County*. Rochester, 1937.

Wrong, George M. *Canada and the American Revolution*. New York: Macmillan, 1935.

Index

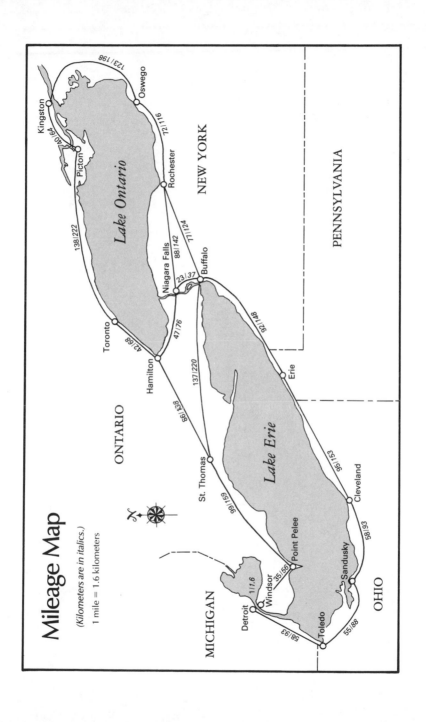

Mileage Map

(Kilometers are in italics.)

1 mile = 1.6 kilometers

ONTARIO

Lake Ontario

Kingston

Picton

Oswego · 123 / 198

72 / 116

Rochester

138 / 222

Niagara Falls · 88 / 142

71 / 124

Buffalo

23 / 37

47 / 76

42 / 68

Toronto

Hamilton

92 / 148

NEW YORK

PENNSYLVANIA

Erie

137 / 220

86 / 138

St. Thomas

Lake Erie

95 / 153

Cleveland

99 / 169

Point Pelee · 35 / 56

58 / 93

Sandusky

MICHIGAN

Detroit · 1 / 1.6

Windsor

58 / 93

Toledo · 55 / 88

OHIO

Cover photographs:
  Niagara Falls © *Farrell Grehan, Photo Researchers, Inc.*
  Renaissance Center *Courtesy of the Detroit Plaza Hotel*